NC
1479
.B26   Anderson, Anthony.
A57
Cp2   The man who was H.M.
          Bateman

                                19.95

THE MAN WHO WAS
H·M·BATEMAN

THE MAN WHO WAS H·M·BATEMAN

Anthony Anderson

Webb&Bower
EXETER, ENGLAND

Published in Great Britain 1982 by
Webb & Bower (Publishers) Limited
9 Colleton Crescent, Exeter, Devon EX2 4BY

Designed by Peter Wrigley

British Library Cataloguing in Publication Data
Anderson, Anthony
    The man who was H. M. Bateman
    1. Bateman, H. M. 2. Cartoonists—England—
Biography
I. Title
741.5′942   NC1479.B/
    ISBN 0-906671-57-4

Typeset in Great Britain by Keyspools Limited,
Golborne, Lancashire

Printed and bound in Hong Kong by Mandarin Offset
International Limited

Contents

PREFACE

'Humour to the humorist is a very solemn business.'

While researching the material for this book, I came across an old plastic
bag filled with little blue diaries[1]. With some excitement I opened one. It
read:

April 2	*Phlegm.*
April 9	*Payed Sunday papers, 3/9.*
June 1	*One pill in night.*
July 23	*Had a cold.*
September 5	*Phlegm.*
December 19	*Very wet and cold.*

I opened another.

February 24	*New batteries.*
August 24	*To Exeter.*
December 13	*Very wheezy. One pill night. Improved midday. Walked to post.*
December 17	*Took pill.*

Much to my disappointment, all the diaries – most of them dating
from the 1960s, when Bateman was more than seventy years old – followed
the same pattern. However, they did reveal something of Bateman's
character which later became most apparent. He was very reticent,
unwilling to talk about himself – even to himself – in any revealing way,
and he was extremely anxious about his health. He was also somewhat
egocentric.

It has become almost axiomatic that great humorists, comedians,
clowns, and others in the business of making people laugh, are often
themselves rather serious, sad, even tragic figures. Humorous artists and
cartoonists are no exception. Surprisingly often the great cartoonists of the
past seem to have been, in contrast to their work, introverted and
uncertain beings, whose lives were full of difficulty. In his *History of
'Punch'*, R. G. G. Price wrote that 'There was an odd tendency for the
leading *Punch* artists to be reserved, sad men.'[2] He mentions especially

Leech, and also Tenniel, who was 'a shy man worried about his health.'
More recently there was Pont (Graham Laidier), a quite brilliant and
much overlooked cartoonist, who died aged only thirty-two, in 1940, of
poliomyelitis. He was described by his biographer, Bernard Hollowood, as
'reserved and shy,'[3] and his life had some remarkable parallels with
Bateman's: he had few adventures except in his mind, suffered from
illness, went to Devon to convalesce, eventually left England for the winter
months, and was, like Bateman, to a remarkable degree lacking in a sense
of humour.

Even some of those cartoonists who lived a much more vivid and
extrovert life than Leech, Tenniel, Pont, or Bateman, lived often near to
tragedy. One thinks especially of Phil May, who, despite a devoted wife,
many friends, and an overtly happy existence, had a terrible compulsion to
drink himself to death, which feat he achieved at the age of thirty-nine and
weight of five stone.

Bateman was a far more careful type, and managed, much to his own
surprise, to live to eighty-three, harbouring his resources, both physical
and financial, with some skill. In this as in most other ways he was in
personality Phil May's complete opposite. However, the one thing which
links the two – indeed all good humorists – together, was their serious
approach to their work. Bateman himself wrote in 1949 that 'Humorous
drawing to the humorous artist is a very serious business,' and John Lewis,
Heath Robinson's biographer, restated the axiom in almost the same
words: 'Humour to the humorist is a very solemn business.'[4] He also
quoted Heath Robinson himself, who wrote, 'At the slightest hint that the
artist was amused the delicate fabric of humour would fade away.'

One might then conclude that the profession of humour demands a
great seriousness, that part of the humour is achieved by the artist's
solemn approach to the silly, funny and peculiar. It is also true that in some
cases – in Bateman's certainly – the ability to approach the humorous in
this way demanded (and perhaps provoked) a certain dryness in the
personality of the artist. This is the central and characteristic incongruity
of Bateman's life and personality: that a man who was constantly
described by those who met him as earnest, serious, even sad, but never as
humorous, indeed never giving any real evidence of a humorous
disposition except through his work, should have become such a brilliant
humorist. Of course, his work was not only funny in the most obvious
sense. One of his great achievements was to broaden the horizons of his art,
to admit the surreal, the ironic and cynical into the good-humoured but
often rather predictable pages of the humorous magazines. However,
while his work constantly gives evidence of a sharp and original sense of
humour, his life gives hardly any.

That he was a reticent and shy man leaves certain problems, largely
that there does not exist a great deal of day-to-day information especially
for the artist's early and most productive years. It is true that he wrote an
autobiography[5] – I have drawn from it extensively – but in many ways it is
rather a disappointment, like the diaries, being mostly anecdotal, and
giving away little about the man himself. The most revealing of all the
material that Bateman left behind is his work – the hundreds of drawings,
cartoons and paintings which tell their own story of development and

achievement. Almost as a corollary to his public reticence, his cartoons were often considerably informed by his own feelings, by situations that had really occurred, and by people he knew. To a much greater degree than one might have supposed, his cartoons offer a history not only of his times but of himself.

In arriving at my picture of the artist I am greatly indebted to his wife, Mrs Brenda Bateman, and daughters, Diana Willis and Monica Pine. They have helped and encouraged me throughout. Indeed, without the collection of cartoons, writings, and other materials in the possession and care of Mrs Diana Willis the book would not have been possible. It was upon her instigation that I undertook this project.

I should also thank for their help Mr David Cuppleditch, author of *The London Sketch Club*, *The John Hassall Lifestyle* and *Phil May*[6], whose long letters dealt patiently with my questions; Mr R. G. G. Price, author of *A History of 'Punch'*, whose suggestions led in many fruitful directions; Mr T. H. H. Hancock, historian of the Chelsea Arts Club; the secretaries of the London Sketch Club and Chelsea Arts Club for allowing me to look at their material; and Mr John Jensen, cartoonist and historian of the cartoon, editor of *The Man Who . . . and other drawings*[7], and great admirer of Bateman's work, for his reading of the proofs of these texts, and for his many helpful suggestions.

I
DEVELOPING THE ART

Henry Charles Bateman, the artist's father, was the son of a hotel keeper who had been a salesman before he married a widow with an establishment in Dover Street, Piccadilly. Both his parents dying early, Henry Charles left the country with a small inheritance, and in 1878, aged twenty-one, arrived in Australia to make his fortune. He bought a homestead called Moss Vale in Sutton Forest, a small village not far from Goulburn, where he lived a hard outdoor life as a cattle man. Australia still had a kind of wild west, and Goulburn was a happy hunting ground for the wildcat promoter and speculator. Mining companies claimed and counter-claimed, and a monthly gold escort left the town for Sydney, often in conditions of danger. Ex-convicts and disappointed gold-rush men made life hazardous. Coaches were robbed, and in the Goulburn district alone some twenty men were killed by these so-called 'bushrangers' during the 1870s.

HENRY CHARLES BATEMAN,
the artist's father.

Though the family left Australia when the artist was only eighteen months old, Bateman's father had for him such glamorous associations throughout his childhood. On the lawn of their suburban house in London he would teach his young son to use a stock-whip, and entertained him with stories of adventure. Bateman later wrote, 'There were times when he literally lived in the saddle for days or even weeks on end, and some of his less robust relations at home in England referred to him as "the bushranger." But it must have been a glorious life.'

Although Bateman admired his father's manliness, he was nearer to his mother, who exerted a strong hold upon him throughout her life. His father had returned to England briefly in 1885, married, and taken his wife back to Australia in that same year. Rose Mayo, born in 1864, was the daughter of a building contractor who lived in Brixton Road, Lambeth, London. Though she showed no particular talent herself, there was some leaning in her family towards the arts: her niece, Daphne Mayo, who also emigrated to Australia, became a successful sculptress. Certainly her own children were encouraged to develop their skills from an early age, and her daughter, Phyllis, the only other child, born in 1890, became an excellent pianist.

H. M. BATEMAN.

Henry Mayo Bateman, known to his family and close friends as Binks, was born at Moss Vale on February 15, 1887. When he eventually returned to the place of his birth some fifty years later, on a dreary rainy day, he found only piles of stones – he described the visit as 'something of a washout.'[1] The Australian adventure had been cut short by his mother, who insisted after his birth that they return to London and civilization. In this, as in other matters, her strong will and determination were decisive, and Bateman senior was forced to settle down to a life of trade. He bought

ROSE MAYO,
the artist's mother.

PHYLLIS BATEMAN,
the artist's sister.

Opposite:
THE FRONT PAGE OF *CHIPS*.
January 1900.
One of the comics Bateman
read as a young boy.

an export packing business in Golden Heart Wharf, Upper Thames Street, and moved his family first to a house in Romford, and then, after a little while, to 36 Therapia Road, Honor Oak, South East London, a Victorian terraced house in a suburban street which he called, nostalgically, Moss Vale, and where they remained until 1905.

Bateman's earliest recollections of their life here were dominated by the devoted but sometimes severe figure of his mother. In a highly untypical scene in his autobiography he recalled his very first memory, a beating, in which he had suffered the indignity of having his trousers pulled down, and blows fell to the incantation of his mother's 'you naughty, *naughty* boy.' It was she who always administered such punishment – his father never beat him. The relationship between mother and son was nevertheless close, and if he was a little frightened of her he also respected her. Though his early sketch-books are dotted with caricatures of his father and sister, he never caricatured his mother in them: she was sacrosanct.

From an early age, he was always drawing, and producing, perhaps as many children do but with greater consistency, funny drawings that told stories. In this, like other cartoonists of his time, he was greatly influenced by the comic papers which were becoming popular towards the end of the nineteenth century. The first comic, and prototype for comics to come, appeared in 1874. It was called *Funny Folks*, was printed weekly in large format and was intended for adults. The idea that there should be a funny paper for children did not take hold until some years later, when Alfred Harmsworth included a junior section in *Puck*[2], which gradually took over the entire comic. (It was also the first to be printed in colour: 1904.) One of the most popular of all was *Chips*, which appeared every Thursday, price one halfpenny, and recounted the adventures of those ancestral heroes of the comic strip, Weary Willie, Gussie the Flea, and Tired Tim.

David Low, the great political cartoonist, could not have evolved a style more different from Bateman's, but he acknowledged the same early debt. 'I do not remember,' he wrote, 'when my interest in drawing began, but it was given direction by the halfpenny comics, *Chips*, *Comic Cuts*, *Larks*, *Funny Wonder*, *The Big Budget*.'[3] Bateman read these comics avidly, and almost echoed Low's words: 'the big one was *Ally Sloper's Half-Holiday*, everyone grew up with that one. It came out on Saturday and I think it was a halfpenny. Then there was *Boy's Own Paper*, *Chums* and *Chips*. There was *Comic Cuts* and a lively thing called *Fun*, which our father used to take. It was wonderful, frightfully good, frightfully funny. And of course there was always *Punch*.'[4] It is interesting that Bateman should have remembered *Fun* with such enthusiasm, because his earliest surviving drawings took the form of a little booklet produced in imitation of that magazine when he was about ten years old.

He had obviously developed a rather keen critical eye at an early age, for though the jokes now seem absolutely dreadful, *Fun* did maintain a noticeably higher standard of drawing than most comics, and the quality of reproduction was unusually good.[5]

Though indebted to the comics of the 1890s, Bateman soon looked to his immediate environment for material for his drawings. He attended a large private school in Forest Hill, near his home, and showed no

No. 488. Vol. XVIII. (New Series.) [Entered at Stationers' Hall.] PRICE ONE HALFPENNY. [Transmission Abroad at Book Rates.] January 6, 1900.

HOW WEARY WILLY, TIRED TIM, AND GUSSY THE FLEA COMMENCED THE NEW YEAR.

1. Clocks were striking 1 a.m. on New Year's Day, when three cloaked figures quietly crept into Chips office. "Stewed tripe and onions!" yelled Bottles, "wot funny fings are blown in by the wind when we leaves the door open! Say, boss! tell 'em we don't want any catsmeat to-day; and if they wants a bath, the dust-heap is just turning round the corner."

2. "Behold!" yelled the strange merchants, as they threw off their disguise; "be e-hold we say, you lop-eared, goggle-e-ed knockpots! We 'ave come for justice to be did; or, in other words, we have come to knock the stuffing out of yer wes-kits." "That's so!" piped the Flea, "and we has come for ber-lud. Ho, ho!" "'Ello! Wot's up?" sniffed Bottles's bull-pup, as it woke up suddenly.

3. "Yow! Oo-oh! Spooth! Boomp! At last, villin, I've got ye! Die like a traitor that you isn't!" yelled Tim, as he peppered Chips. "I'll teach yer to laugh at us, you pigeon-chested monster-osity!" cried Willy. Whack! "'Ere! wot's the game?" asked the Fighting Editor, as he put his features round the door. "Who wants killing?"

4. "I don't!" squeaked Tim. "So git orf me windpipe! Wough!" "Mother, is the earthquake over?" gurgled Willy, "'cos I've got the wiffle-woffles in me flim-flam!" "Per-lice!" piped the Flea; "this tyke is the rudest pusson I've ever tasted! Stow it, when I tells you! S-q-u-e-a-k!"

5. "Yes, me lord!" said old Chips to the beak; "these low-down ruffians tried to make orphums of my wife and children! What d'ye think of it?" "Disgraceful!" answered the judge, "and most vulgar to biff the funniest Editor in the World. Seven days on bread and water, without the option of a chew of bacoy."

6. "Oh! you pretty blighters!" blubbered Gussy the Flea. "This is seeing life, and commencing the New Year well, is it? If I could only get me stinger near yer feelings I'd make yer hop!" "Gerrout!" groaned Willy. "Some people is never satisfied. 'Ere's a nice week's holiday, and ye're grumbling already! Wot more d'ye want?"

(Continued in next Thursday's "Chips." One Halfpenny.)

Above:
'ILS FUMENT. ILS SONT ARRÊTÉS.'
Early drawing from school,
c. 1900.

Right:
BATEMAN'S *FUN*
His earliest surviving
drawing, *c*. 1897.

exceptional aptitude for academic life; but he would cover the backs of his exercise books with drawings illustrating the lessons he was suffering.

'Drawing,' he said, 'was beginning to run strongly through every phase of my young life. At every available moment I was drawing something and every fresh experience served as a subject for a sketch.' Soon, drawing on the backs of used pieces of paper, though a practice he returned to later in life, no longer signified a sufficient commitment, and he started to buy the first of the many sketch-books he was to fill throughout his career.

AFTER THE MATCH.

his first publication.

An obviously blossoming talent make these early sketch-books delightful, various and vivid. They are filled with schoolboy matter: a great deal of sport, other pupils, masters, whimsical and energetic caricatures. Phyllis was a frequent butt, and being the sister of a budding cartoonist with a slightly acid eye must have been trying at times.

Though a rather frail child, Bateman displayed a quality of enthusiasm that made up for the greater physical robustness of his schoolfellows. As a sportsman he lacked the gregariousness that gives the true 'team spirit,' but it was quite clear that whatever the activity he undertook he would devote himself to it body and soul. He developed a tenacity that delighted in undertaking the difficult, and an almost scientific curiosity in experiencing for himself those encounters which provided the drama for his cartoons. Thus one of his favourite pastimes was boxing, at which he never really excelled, and through which he often sustained considerable injuries to his nose, which bled rather easily and, being rather large – he was sensitive about this – offered an excellent target. He and a far more skilled and beefy companion would retire to an empty room at the top of his house and battle away in the most amiable fashion until the blood started to flow, at which point the fighting ceased and Bateman would use the stream to create funny faces on the bare boards, which presented rather a good and slightly absorbent surface.

Already by the time he was fourteen, in 1901, he had decided upon his future: he would draw for publication. This precocious singleness of purpose was shaped and sustained by two significant events in that same year.

Above:
CARICATURES OF HIS SISTER PHYLLIS, AND FATHER, on holiday at Aldeburgh, *c.* 1903, from the artist's sketch-books.

Above Left:
BATEMAN'S FIRST PUBLISHED DRAWING, produced as a postcard at Forest Hill School. Signed 'Binks'.

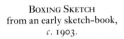

The greatest living English cartoonist – the acknowledged master of the art – was Phil May.[6] The young boy greatly admired him, and tried, as did legions of others, to imitate his bold and clear style. Bateman's mother, who had watched her young son's growing interest and skill, and would often sit and model for him patiently in the evenings after school, turned her sympathetic attendance upon his early talent in a more positive and practical direction. Of a decisive personality, and having conceived considerable ambitions for him, she sent May a selection of his work, with a letter asking for advice about his future direction. May replied most kindly.

Madam

I have looked at your boy's drawings with a good deal of interest, and think he promises to develop a talent for comic draughtsmanship. Of course he will have to go through the drudgery of a year or so's schooling to perfect his drawing. It is difficult to advise as to what particular line of study the youngster should take up, unless you know him. Boys are so different, and possibly the routine of some schools might dishearten him.

However I think you might let him go on as he is for, say, another year. Then send him to the Westminster School of Art and my friend Mr Mouat Loudan will do everything that possibly can be done to develop his talents without interfering with his originality.

I have to apologise for not having answered sooner, but I have so many things to do and must take everything in its turn, otherwise I should get into a hopeless muddle.

I am, Madam

Yours faithfully

Phil May.[7]

It is sad to note that Phil May was at this time a very ill man, dying of cirrhosis of the liver, which killed him in 1903, yet he found the time and had the goodness to reply with consideration to an unknown lady soliciting advice on behalf of her teenage son. Such was the respect his opinion commanded that his advice was followed implicitly, and Bateman did indeed go to the Westminster.

The other great event of 1901 for the young artist was the exhibition of black-and-white art at the Victoria and Albert Museum in London. Black-and-white was the trade jargon and popular term for almost all illustrative work, and illustrative artists in general were known as 'black-and-white men.' The reason for this, obviously enough, was that most illustrative work was reproduced only in black and white, and therefore to a large extent artists were restricted in their original work to whatever they could achieve through the medium of pen or pencil. However, by 1901 the whole printing industry had undergone tremendous expansion and revolution through technological change.

Before the 1880s, a drawing was reproduced by engraving on wood. The artist had to send his work to the engraver – unless he drew directly on to the block himself – and the original work would then be cut up, and as a result of course destroyed, as the engraver cut his lines round the lines of the drawing and on to the wood. This could be a disturbing process for the artist to witness, especially since the resulting 'copy' was completely at the mercy of the engraver's skill, and often highly inaccurate. Furthermore, the line of the sharp knife or engraving tool on wood was far less flexible and fluid than the line of an artist's pen or pencil upon paper, and gave to the reproduction that rather stiff and wooden feeling one associates with the work of artists such as Leech and Tenniel, which seems to fit so beautifully the formality and stiffness of Victorian life, the medium reflecting something of the personality of the age. There also developed, because of the often pressing need to get the artists' work into print quickly, partly brought on by the very slowness of the method itself and partly by the almost statutory panic caused by having to get things ready for press by a certain deadline, the seemingly peculiar but time-saving custom of dividing the block up into little squares and sharing these out among the team of engravers within the workshop. The master engraver would then join them all up again and try to make sure there were no radical differences between the parts. Bateman's friend and perhaps greatest rival in popularity as a humorous artist, William Heath Robinson, came from a whole family of artists and illustrators, and remembered his uncle working directly on to the block itself, and having to send off each little square as he completed it, so that the engravers could get to work quickly.[8]

If the engraver had views which did not conform to the artist's original intentions, the results could be catastrophic. Dante Gabriel Rossetti had terrible troubles with the Dalziel brothers over his illustrations for Tennyson's 'In Memoriam,' and wrote to W. Bell-Scott that he had 'designed five blocks for Tennyson, save seven which are still cutting and maiming. It is a thankless task, after a fortnight's work my block goes to the engraver, like Agag, and is hewn to pieces before the Lord Harry.'[9] He then continued with an address to the Dalziels.

CARICATURES OF THE ARTIST'S SISTER PHYLLIS, AND HIS FATHER, from an early sketch-book, c. 1903.

O woodman spare that block,
O gash not anyhow!
It took ten days by clock
I'd fain protect it now.

Chorus: Wild laughter from Dalziel's workshop.

Rossetti was a great perfectionist; in fact, despite all the difficulties, the Dalziel brothers were generally highly respected, and played a great part in helping to encourage that 'remarkable outburst of beautiful design for the illustration of books and periodicals, the work of the chief artists of the day which came to be specially distinguished in the history of Art as "the Sixties."' The Sixties then formed the first part of the exhibition. Much of the work was brilliant, but, as David Low put it, 'generally speaking all had had to work "with the wood," and their drawings could not escape a certain family resemblance imposed by the technique of the graver's tools.'[10]

The other great period of work represented was the 1890s, and here, though a link was formed between the old and the new by men like Keene and du Maurier, a great difference was at once apparent. The heroes of the 'new wave,' Phil May and Aubrey Beardsley had never had to work for the engraver, and their work was astonishingly free. A great part of this stylistic freedom was due to the replacement during the 1880s of the woodblock method of reproduction by the wonderful new development of photo-process engraving,[11] a mechanical (rather than manual) method of reproduction, which gave far greater accuracy and was far quicker and cheaper. The changeover from the earlier to the later method had been rapid. In 1888, the *Illustrated London News* included twenty-six pictures: seventeen were wood engravings, nine process blocks. In 1901, the same magazine could reproduce fifty pictures, all of them by process block. Even *Punch*, 'the most conservative of papers in keeping to the old method,' resisted the claims of process work until 1892, but by the time of the Victoria and Albert exhibition only the weekly full-page leading cartoon was engraved in wood.[12] It was this technological revolution which 'led to the enormous increase in the number of illustrated books and journals,' feeding a print hungry public, and the great revival in black-and-white drawing which the exhibition celebrated. It 'summed up on a national scale the extraordinary fecundity and originality of magazine and book illustration from 1890.'[13] It was in this atmosphere of excitement, of expansion, and of opportunity, that the young Bateman decided to 'draw for publication.' He could not have done so at a more propitious time.

PUBLICATION AND A HELPING HAND

The only major obstacle facing Bateman across his chosen path was his father's opposition. Although his father was a poor match for his mother, once she had come to a decision, the question of the boy's future was undoubtedly one upon which the full force of his role as master of the family's affairs could be brought, and he was determined that his son should follow him into the business. He thought art an effeminate occupation. The relationship between father and mother was becoming increasingly difficult, and arguments about their son's career helped to drive his father into a more and more isolated position, as mother and son squared ranks against him.

Shortly after Bateman's sixteenth birthday, however, when the time for decision came, his father's attitude had turned from implacable opposition to helpful acquiescence. The boy was to go after all, just as Phil May had advised, to Mr Mouat Loudan at the Westminster – and his father would finance him entirely. The reason for this about-turn was not simply that Bateman senior had collapsed under pressure, but that by the middle of 1903 his son had to some extent proved himself.

He had, since the start of the previous year, managed to place a few of his cartoons in the halfpenny weekly comic papers, and from late in 1902 he began to do so on a regular basis. Indeed, between January and August 1903 he was placing a cartoon every fortnight, which must have given considerable excitement to a boy of his age. The fact that he seemed

PRIDE GOES BEFORE A FALL.

" Oh, yes, Miss Trimm, the figure is quite easy. You just go like that, and – " That !

PUBLISHED IN *SCRAPS* NO 1013.
10 January 1903.

capable of earning an income, however small, impressed his father very favourably, and perhaps he also recognized in the boy a certain canny instinct for the market. The work that he sent off to *Scraps*, *Chips* and *Comic Life* was in many respects less interesting and less mature than the work in his sketch-books over the same period. He understood the tone of these papers, and gave them what they wanted: what would fit in.

In the summer of 1903, then, Bateman left Forest Hill School and became an art student. Already with some commercial experience, and a hard-won family battle behind him, he set off for the Westminster School of Art, at 18 Tufton Street, Deans Yard, Westminster, part of the old Architectural Museum. The instructors were Mr Mouat Loudan, Mr J. Holgate and Mr F. E. Schenck. As was usual in those days,[1] men and women were instructed separately, the ladies paying five shillings more for the extra care necessary in supervising their struggles with the human body. The fees for men in the life class were £2.10s. per term, payable in advance, but Bateman, who was considered too young for the life classes, was set to drawing casts, which was much cheaper, costing his father only £1.5s. In the cast room, with only one other youthful companion, he fast approached a state nearing boredom: here he sat among the lifeless, while all around him, and indeed within, he sensed excitement. These were not the stirring times he had foreseen, and within nine months he had decided to leave the Westminster, and transfer to the Goldsmith Institute, at New Cross, which had a rather more liberal approach. Despite this, his memories of the Westminster were on the whole fond ones. He came later to appreciate the discipline of having drawn from casts – and it was, after all, his first real exposure to the artistic life.

The old Westminster was arranged on four floors with galleries running round a big square courtyard, the whole being covered over with a glass roof. Off the galleries were the various rooms which made up the school, the galleries themselves being filled with specimens of architecture which gave the whole place the air of a museum, which of course it was.

The men's life-room was on the ground floor and the women's was on the top. Sometimes I and my stable companion in the cast-room would go out for a breather on our gallery on the first floor and speculate at a respectful distance upon the students who might be out during their model's hourly rest. As a matter of fact we soon learnt the usual times for the rests and we went out then ourselves if we wanted to make sure of seeing the lions and lionesses sunning themselves. There is always something racy about a young girl art student, and some of those at the old Westminster came right up to expectation by smoking cigarettes, a thing almost depraved in its advancement for those days. . . .

Before I had qualified at the Westminster to leave the casts and 'draw from the nude,' for one reason or another I transferred to the Goldsmith Institute at New Cross. Here I worked all day and often at evening classes as well. . . .

I worked in big classes, frequently mixed, instead of being shut up in a room with only an occasional companion, and the change to me proved stimulating.

'STRATEGY OUTWITS THE LAW'
published in *The Royal*,
November 1904.

While he studied, he continued to work away at his cartoons, and it was the principal of the Goldsmith Institute, Frank Marriot, who, noticing that between the careful drawings from life in the boy's sketch-books were pages covered in 'comical faces and exaggerated figures,' helped Bateman towards his first commission – an advertisement for a firm of paper manufacturers – and gave him the necessary encouragement and advice.

His real chance, however, came by way of a fellow student, the sister of Shackleton the explorer. At this time, early in 1904, Shackleton was working for the publishers, C. A. Pearson, and through him, and on the basis of a portfolio of humorous drawings, Bateman was given a contract for some ten cartoons and two illustrations for stories in *The Royal* magazine. Pearson were later to publish many of his cartoons in their own *Pearson's Weekly*, so this was the start of a useful association, but the important point to Bateman at the time was that by publishing in *The Royal* he raised himself above the level of the comics and their very basic requirements.

The Royal came out monthly, at fourpence, and was devoted to lighthearted stories of adventure and romance with titles such as 'The Perils of the High Peaks,' or 'Submarined,' and 'true-life' accounts such as 'The Greatest Bicycle Feat in the World.' There were also occasional pieces of work of a really high standard by an author such as Maupassant. As was customary in almost every magazine at the time, a large section was devoted to the stage, adorned with photographs of leading actors and actresses, and discussions of their latest triumphs, both artistic and personal, and, of course, there were cartoons, by artists such as Harry Rountree, Tom Browne, and Lawson Wood, men Bateman would soon know personally.

His own drawings, while they were again produced with a clear understanding of the market, here represent a considerable advance upon his pre-art school publications, and so self-assured is their draughtsmanship that they could easily be taken for the work of a mature artist.

This success with *The Royal* was soon followed by another with *The Tatler*, a far more prestigious magazine, and one not given to publishing the work of the very young. Bateman was more than happy.

> It was in 1904 that I had the courage to try my work on the sixpenny ... weeklies, and I actually managed to place some things with *The Tatler*, the very paper with which I am still most closely associated and for which I must always have an abiding affection and respect. *The Tatler* was founded by the late Clement Shorter[2], and he and his sub-editor, Arthur Croxton, were most encouraging to me. At first they would pick one out of several I tried with them and for which I believe they paid me a guinea, but after a while I attempted a series and drew some comic renderings of lines taken from the Lays of Ancient Rome. Mostly I had been sending my things in by post, as I had not the time to hawk them round myself, but this set I thought I had better take up to the office in person.
>
> There were five of them and two other oddments which I had the cheek to try all at once, and I shall never forget the thrill I experienced when word came out to me in the waiting-room that Mr Shorter would use them all and would like to see some more!

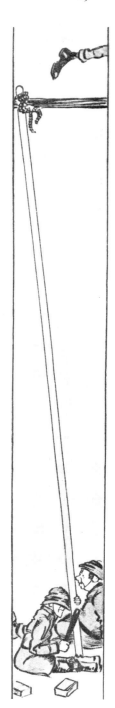

Intoxicated, almost blind with excitement, I got out of the building and for half an hour I galloped through the network of streets which lay around the *Tatler* offices, until, without any idea of the direction in which I had been running, I found myself back again in the entrance to the building.

Seven whole guineas at one fell swoop! Ye Gods! I felt as if I should burst.

'LAYS OF ANCIENT ROME
RE-ILLUSTRATED – NO III.'
Published in *The Tatler*,
No 177, 16 November 1904.
'With bright frank brow that
had not learned to blush at
gaze of man – *Virginia*'.

These cartoons appeared between August 1904 and February 1905, and there were, in fact, ten 'Lays of Ancient Rome Re-illustrated,' and six others. The idea of illustrating lines from Macaulay's famous poem, which every schoolboy learnt by heart, was a good but not original one. Bateman was really following a cartoon convention most notable perhaps in Phil May's illustrations of lines from Shakespeare, which had appeared in *The Sketch* and in *Punch* during 1902.[3] Though the style of draughtsmanship in these cartoons is a synthesis of prevailing cartoon styles, and the humour too comes from a well-worn mould, these were not merely imitations, and the self-assurance of the finished product is remarkable in a sixteen-year-old.

This success was a wonderful confirmation and encouragement, but with the increasing demands now made upon his time, Bateman, already rather a reserved and solitary boy, was thrown farther back upon himself. His father and his mother, the one puzzled, the other eager, could not provide the necessary stimulus, nor could they contribute to his work in any active way. At this moment he badly needed the friendship and advice of someone who had been through something of his particular struggle, whose understanding was based upon similar experience. Through some of his fellow students at the Westminster he found the right man.

John Hassall was, in 1904, at the peak of his career as one of the leading poster artists and illustrators of the day. He was thirty-five years old, a family man, with three children from his first wife, who had died tragically in childbirth, and a young and lovely second wife, who was to give him three more. He was young enough to be companionable, and old enough to have authority, and he had about him the visible signs of success: a large house in Kensington, a happy family behind him, and, most importantly, a studio full of work. In great demand, he would work at many commissions and projects all at once, allowing any admiring youngsters who were around to lend a helping hand. He was enormously impressive to Bateman, not only because he was so prolific but also because he had the force of personality to match his great energy as an artist. He was very handsome, well built, tall and expansive, and Bateman, who was rather small and shy, could in all senses look up to him. It was only because there was already formed a hard and stubborn core of ego within that the younger artist was not completely submerged by Hassall's presence and influence. As it was, he remembered years later that Hassall had been 'a god' to him, and he spoke of youngsters like himself going round to Hassall's busy studio, a place of perpetual fascination, and 'warming themselves in his radiance.'

Hassall's influence upon Bateman was diffuse and personal more than artistic. Though some of his work at this time reflects Hassall's style and approach, much does not, and Bateman's relationship with him was never a matter of unquestioning discipleship. The artistic lessons he learnt from Hassall were soon assimilated or superceded by his own fast-forming individuality of style. They were basically anyway more suited to poster art, which never much interested Bateman – though he could be quite successful at it – namely, a broad simplicity, with one large area of tone or colour put flatly beside another contrasting one, and a 'certain breezy manliness,' as a critic in *The Studio* put it.[4] The personalities of the two men were so completely different, so opposite, and their work so characteristic of their personalities, that Bateman could never fruitfully have developed upon the same lines. The extrovert, the introvert; the public, the private; the simple, the complex. Hassall's strengths were also his weaknesses: bold, broad and vivid, his work lacked 'anything feminine or delicate. We miss partly on this account the charm of subtlety: it is so very straightforward in execution, and in intention so direct.'[5]

Hassall, however, introduced Bateman to a whole new world. He was a convivial and immensely popular man, who knew most of the black-and-white illustrators, the cartoonists, and the poster artists, many of whom would visit his studio. Through Hassall and his friends, Bateman was put in touch with the London art clubs, and most particularly the Sketch Club, which was Hassall's own favourite. Though he was not elected a member until 1907 – he was, after all, still only seventeen: perhaps a little too young for all the drinking and smoking – Bateman soon got to know many of the artists who frequented it. (See chapter 5.)

The most important service Hassall did for the young artist was to take him and point him in the right direction at a crucial stage in his career – just as Phil May had done, from a greater remove, back in 1901. He advised Bateman to leave the Goldsmith Institute and enrol as a student with his own old tutor, a Dutch painter, Charles Van Havermaet, who had just come over from Holland and taken a studio in Earls Court, close to Olympia.

Hassall's advice was based not only upon his own experience but upon what amounted to almost a tradition of the period. A great many of the best-known illustrators and cartoonists had spent their formative years in Holland or France, studying at some currently popular studio or in a painting academy, and had therefore laid solid foundations in traditional painting method before starting commercial careers.[6] Many of these commercial artists had aspirations as serious painters which never left them, and, like Hassall himself, continued to submit work to the Royal Academy or Royal Society of Watercolourists throughout their lives. Hassall, on the advice of his friend Dudley Hardy, had gone, as Hardy had done before him, to study in Paris and Antwerp, and, quite apart from the formal training he received, came into contact with new continental ideas and styles. Hassall and Hardy between them, greatly influenced by Cheret, brought the poster to England, and established something of a school of poster artists.[7]

So Hassall's advice to Bateman showed the young man the way to acquire something of the flavour and excitement of a continental studio without having actually to leave the country, and, while providing a proper introduction to painting, would put him under the supervision of the man who, Hassall often said, had been responsible for a great deal of his own success. Bateman did not delay, and in the early part of 1905 he left the Goldsmith Institute and went to Van Havermaet's studio, where he remained for nearly three years.

3
COLOUR AND LINE

Bateman's years at Van Havermaet's studio were busy ones. He continued to work hard at academic drawing, often in charcoal, to learn about watercolour and oil paint, and he also bombarded the London magazines with a stream of cartoons. His family moved, at the beginning of 1905, to 2 Bonneville Road, Clapham Common, a far larger house, where he had his own studio at the very top. Then, after studying all day at Van Havermaet's, starting at nine in the morning and coming home often late in the evening, he would retire to his room to work away at his cartoons, his rate of production accelerating steadily as he discovered a seemingly insatiable market.

Of all the things he learnt from Van Havermaet he appreciated most the careful and rigorous instruction in drawing which proved of 'incalculable value' to him. But the daily enjoyment he found in going to the studio had much to do with eating boiled eggs out of candlesticks and not doing the washing up. He loved the atmosphere of the big, sparsely furnished old house, and the feeling that this was the 'proper way, the traditional way for an artist to live.'[1]

In August 1905, having already placed drawings with *The Sketch*, *London Opinion* and *The Bystander* (which was eventually taken over by *The Tatler*) – all of them magazines that continued to publish his work for many years – he was given his first full-page cartoon. It was published in *The Sketch*, and others followed each month for the rest of the year.

The Tatler also now gave him regular employment, and he was engaged to illustrate the weekly financial page, in a series that ran for eighteen months. His job was 'to go to Company Meetings and sketch the chairman delivering his annual report. . . . When I was wanted I knocked off my studies for a few hours and went to the City to make notes of my subject, which I worked out afterwards at home. These drawings were not so much caricatures as rather humorous little portraits, but when they first began to appear they were considered sufficiently extravagant, or insulting, as to cause several of the subjects to write letters of protest to *The Tatler*, threatening to stop their subscriptions. However, they soon cooled down when others of their confrères appeared, and actually the series developed into quite a successful little feature of the paper.'

These 'humorous little portraits' owed something to the *portraits chargés* of Max Beerbohm, whom he very much admired, and to those of Fred Lynch, a caricaturist who contributed to *Fun*, but his work was far from settling in one mould. While the portraits for *The Tatler* were an excellent discipline for him, and helped develop an ability to sum up a personality with a few lines of the pencil, Bateman began also to have

'AN AUTHORITY ON NITRATE.'
The Tatler, No 205,
31 May 1905.

'THE APOSTLE OF RETRENCHMENT.'
The Tatler, No 204,
24 May 1905.

confidence in his own imagination and fantasy, and for the first time
allowed his own slightly peculiar vision to dictate the subject matter for his
drawings. He produced a series of seven full-page cartoons for *The Sketch*,
under the general title of 'Hauntings,' which look back to a diversity of
influences, and also contain characteristic elements of his later work, not
only in their design but in their whimsical and surreal logic.

   During 1906 and 1907 many of his cartoons became rather painterly –
hardly surprising considering the nature of his training. He took great care
with his compositions, referring to life whenever he could, one shape
complementing another, the right balance of figures against the right
background, and started to use delicate washes of watercolour for
backgrounds and to give his figures substance. Though he is largely
remembered as a line draughtsman, it is quite clear that Bateman's time as
a student fostered in him an appreciation of space and tone which he soon

Opposite:
HIS FIRST PUBLISHED
FULL-PAGE CARTOON.

WHEN FORCE TRIUMPHS OVER ART.

BURLY NAVVY (*to the little man who has attempted to grapple with him*): Nah, then. A little less er yer joo-jitsoo. D'y'ear?

DRAWN BY H. M. BATEMAN.

put to good use in his cartoons. When P. V. Bradshaw, founder of the Press Art School and a great popularizer of illustrative art,[2] first met Bateman, in 1906, 'at a time when everybody interested in illustration was talking about him,' he found a 'quiet, shy, delicate boy who was much more interested in colour than in line work, and who could only with difficulty be induced to talk about either.'

In the summer of 1906, Bateman contributed some cartoons to a new magazine, *Printers' Pie* – another publication to flourish during this period of productivity and expansion – and was invited to a grand dinner at the Savoy to celebrate its successful start. A photograph of the occasion later appeared in *The Tatler*, and showed him sitting among his fellow contributors, men for the most part twenty or so years older than himself, looking rather pensive in his starched front and white bow-tie. Among his fellow diners were Harold Harmsworth (Lord Rothermere, younger brother of Alfred, Viscount Northcliffe) and C. Arthur Pearson – two of the most dynamic of all Edwardians – as well as established artists, many of whom he had met before, such as Hassall, Cecil Aldin, Raven-Hill, George Belcher, Lewis Baumer and Fred Pegram. Though Clapham and the Savoy were poles apart, his world was beginning to take shape.

Bateman had not, however, outgrown his schoolboy enthusiasms, and at this time he started to take boxing lessons from a former lightweight champion, 'old Bat Mullins . . . the last man to fight with the bare fist,' and also with 'another Professor of the Noble Art and a lightweight champion of Great Britain, whose gymnasium, if it can be called that, lay behind a tavern at the Elephant and Castle. To get to his room it was necessary to pass through the bar, which occupied about twenty minutes, and to get back to the street took still longer, and cost more, as he strove to impress upon me the need for keeping a straight left. One day the professor brought his son to spar with me as a little change. The son had not the same carefully modulated touch as his sire. He was thoroughly workmanlike, though, and when they brought me round his father told me with pride that the lad was in training for the championship.'

Boxing had not long been legalized, and at this time it still had something of the exciting flavour of bear-baiting or cock-fighting. Bateman would sometimes take his sketch-book and go down to Deptford, where there was a large boxing ring, and draw the crowds and the fighters. During every holiday, all over England, there were fairs and race meetings, and not least among the attractions were the boxing booths, which invited any plucky spectator to take his pick of the 'professionals' on view, and have a go. Like many Londoners, Bateman escaped for these festivities, and, drawn towards the boxers, he would make sketches and take photographs – a new enthusiasm – which eventually found their way into his cartoons.[3]

Whelk-sellers, racing touts, coconut shies, fattest men in the world – everything became material. He had a real Dickensian love of the way in which character expresses itself through physical appearance. To capture the vivid individuality of these natural performers, Bateman would emphasize or exaggerate their form, but not, as was later the case, in any malign way. The impression is of something believed to be real: the good-humoured grass roots of Edwardian England.

Opposite:
'THE OBSESSION OF THE DINER OUT.'
The Sketch, 6 December 1905. The central figure of the naked man was drawn from a model at Van Havermaet's. The treatment and design owe something perhaps to Beardsley and more especially to S. H. Sime. The separate sections and comments on the main cartoon were to become a special feature of Bateman's cartoons.

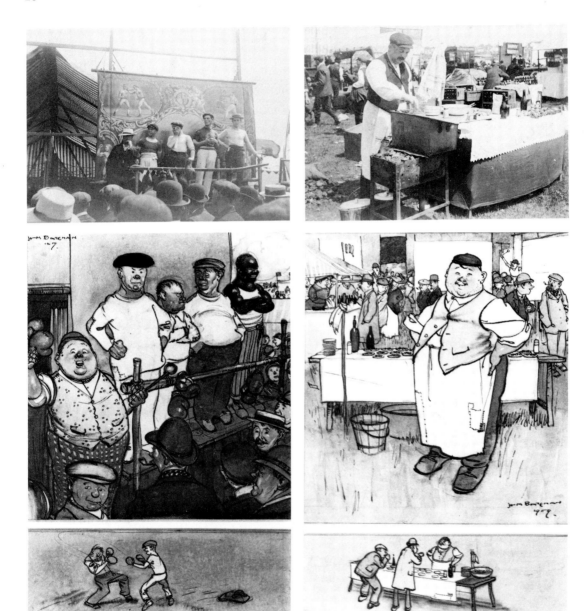

Above:
EARLY EXAMPLES OF BATEMAN'S USE OF PHOTOGRAPHY
as a basis for his cartoons.

Opposite:
'SEASIDE TYPES' – 'DOWN FOR THE DAY.'
London Opinion, 26 June 1909.
The figure in the centre bears a strong resemblance
to the artist's father.

GUESTS AT THE SAVOY DINNER
to celebrate the success of
the magazine *Printers' Pie*.
Bateman is second from left,
centre row. John Hassall is
centre, back row.

Bateman went at least once a year on holiday with his parents, usually
to the seaside, all over the South coast, as far west as Devon and Cornwall,
and sometimes up to Norfolk or Suffolk. They stayed in that kind of
respectable boarding house, or private hotel, which still manages somehow
to exist in places, sticking to the coast like some prehistoric mollusc. From
such a point of safety Bateman ventured forth, pencil in hand, hunting for
'types.'

Types were another cartoon convention, a way of looking at people
that revealed more than just a personality: an essay on class, character,
occupation and predilection, again perhaps most notably exploited earlier
by Phil May. Bateman was to raise the art to new levels, and though he had
not yet developed that characteristic line which embodied a whole world of
nuance (it was not long in coming), his holiday drawings were full of
character and atmosphere.

In 1907, during the summer, the family went down to Dartmouth, and
it was here that he took his photographs of the fair. He also prowled the
beaches filling his sketch-books with old men in deck-chairs, people
fishing, bathing, lounging or reading, and these were duly transformed
into a series of 'Seaside Types,' later published in *London Opinion*. He
wrote that a crowded seaside resort was one of his favourite places in which
to work.

It was also at this time that Bateman started to go abroad for his
holidays. Inspired by Van Havermaet, he made two journeys to Holland,
with his camera, and took what is now a remarkable set of photographs of
Dutch life before the Great War. He went first to Volendam, the fishing
port on the Zuider Zee, and stayed in an inn which seemed to cater
especially for artists. It was like a Bohemian club, with cigars at a penny,
good food and beer, and walls hung with the paintings and sketches of
previous visitors. The Dutch people still wore traditional costume: wide
trousers and tight jerkins for the men, and big petticoats and coifs for the
women – and, of course, wooden clogs. Bateman was delighted by
everything, and this little taste of how different and refreshing things
could be away from home gave him a huge appetite for foreign travel,
which was to play a large part in the course of his life from now on.

Despite such pleasures, all was not well. Deeply introverted, and
constitutionally never strong, he was now working very hard, and his
capacity for work drew upon a supply of nervous energy that needed
careful nurturing and could be suddenly and dramatically drained.
Towards the end of 1907, Bateman was wrestling in earnest with what
seemed to him an awful decision. He knew that he could not stay for ever as
a student with Van Havermaet, and yet during his years with him he had
been encouraged to think that he might make a serious painter, if only he

Saturday Afternoon in
Volendam, 1907.

continued to apply himself. For a long time he could not decide whether he
should in fact try to become a painter or if he was at heart a humorous
artist, and should stop pretending to be otherwise. When he finally made
his decision to leave the shelter of the studio and commit himself to a
career as a cartoonist, the tension and strain within him had become so
great that it was as if a taut wire had been suddenly cut. He collapsed. He
spent his twenty-first birthday in bed at home with a nurse by his side,
suffering from 'nervous exhaustion,' nowadays called a nervous
breakdown, and it was many weeks before he was well again.

He had caught that disease endemic among cartoonists: the desire to
paint serious pictures. It undermined his health as surely as any virus
could have done, and lingered, as viruses do, for a long time. In fact his
decision, made at such cost, never really ended the matter, and when many
years later he gave up regular cartoon work, it was almost with a sense of
relief that he turned back to painting. He had only suppressed the desire,
not resolved it. He was never quite the same after his breakdown; the fear
of a repetition of such a collapse hung over him for years after. He became
something of a hypochondriac, always most anxious about his health.
However, not all its effects were bad ones, and the following year, 1908,
proved to be one of the most creative and seminal in his career. It was the
year in which he made his first major contributions to the art of the cartoon.

4
A NEW APPROACH

Paradoxically, Bateman's nervous breakdown seems to have had a most beneficial and cathartic effect upon his work – as though, all doubts cast aside, he was able to redouble his efforts, and stride out with resolution. First, his commitment deepened through the sheer volume of work he undertook now that he was no longer a student. During 1907, he had placed some forty full cartoons, as well as a number of minor drawings, with London magazines.[1] In 1908, that figure doubled, and by 1909 there were three new Bateman cartoons appearing each week. He kept up this rate of work until the War. He was always meticulous, and often made many preliminary sketches before deciding upon the final version.

But there was not only a quantitative change: there were marked changes in quality and in kind also. The cartoons he had been drawing until now had all been of the 'illustrated joke' variety: underneath the drawing there was a caption – often a few lines of dialogue – which the cartoon served to illustrate. Remove the writing, and the drawing becomes meaningless – the joke lay in the words. Bateman now started to dispense with these words and make the drawing self-explanatory. He discovered – and in so doing changed the English cartoon – that the drawing itself could be funny, that there was such a thing as a 'humorous line.' This can be seen as the next natural step in the liberation of the cartoon, after Phil May started to draw characters who actually reacted to their situation. Phil May's drawing, however, was academic compared to Bateman's, and never managed – nor indeed wanted – to escape from that family resemblance which made up almost a school, or at least an ancestral line, of *Punch* cartoonists.[2] Bateman eventually broke with this line entirely.

It would be untrue to say that suddenly in 1908 Bateman's drawing became inherently humorous, and that it had not been at all so before: there had been a continuous process of change and improvement, a development of characteristic method, which, in retrospect, seems almost an inevitable progression. However, it is very noticeable that during 1908 the explanatory caption or dialogue disappeared from beneath the drawings. Whereas almost all his cartoons during 1907 and before had been illustrated jokes, by 1909 there is hardly one such to be found – and though they do occur from then on, they are very rare.

The qualitative change was that he now really started to make emotion the subject of his cartoons, and the characters became actors, expressing feeling, rather than illustrations to an idea. His drawings became much more intense or charged than before. He freed himself from the conventional stillness of cartoon figures and, in his own words, 'went mad on paper.'

MUSIC HALL SKETCHES
from the artist's sketch-books,
c. 1908.

WITHIN THIS UNTITLED CARTOON
there is a nice confrontation
of styles: the lady
representing the shocked but
still decorous old style
confronted by the over-emotional
gentleman with his twisting
trouser legs of the new
style.

It is tempting to see a direct causal link between this and his
breakdown, and obviously some intellectual reorganization did take place,
but the origin and inspiration for this new approach and technique lay not
so much within the sphere of his own perturbations as in the daily round of
his experience as a cartoonist.

He now started to take much of his subject matter from the theatre,
and especially from the flourishing music halls and variety houses he loved
to visit. In the winter of 1908, the *Lady's Realm* magazine published a
series of seven cartoons on 'The Intensity of Modern Drama' in which
Bateman's newer and more individual style is at once apparent. His work
has often been described as 'histrionic' or 'melodramatic,' and it is in

Nov. 27, 1907   THE SKETCH.   211

HOITY TOITY!

LADY (*meeting Mary, who was once her servant*): Why, Mary, how are you? Where are you living now?
MARY: Thank you, Mum; I ain't livin' nowheres now – I'm married.

AN OLD-STYLE ILLUSTRATED JOKE cartoon where the caption carries the burden of humour and meaning: 'LADY (*meeting Mary, who was once her servant*): "Why, Mary, how are you? Where are you living now?" MARY: "Thank you, Mum; I ain't livin' nowheres now – I'm married."'

unconscious recognition of the stage as a source of inspiration that these descriptions come.

Bateman took one step farther the actor's personification of emotion by exaggerated expression, and, like an actor, he found his way to this through a sympathetic appreciation of feeling that came not merely from distant observation but through intense and often physical identification with his subject. Though it was usually enough to enact the emotion in his mind's eye in order to set it down on paper he would sometimes sit in front of a mirror and twist his face and body until he found just the right shape to convey the feeling he sought to express. It was a habit he never allowed to become too public – part of the reason perhaps that he demanded

'The Plotters',
from 'The Intensity of
Modern Drama as Drawn in
Seven Acts by H. M. Bateman.'
Lady's Realm, Christmas 1908.

complete privacy when he worked. Years later, not long after he was married, his unsuspecting wife passed by the window of his studio, and there, to her horror, she observed her husband in an awful agony of mind, his features dreadfully contorted. Not wishing to intrude upon such passion, but being naturally disturbed, and not a little curious, she asked him after dinner, with a great air of innocence, how his work was progressing. He told her he was having a terrible time of it and that he just could not capture the right expression for the feeling he was trying to convey. She was much relieved.

For Bateman, the genesis of this new method was a memorable occasion.

On a certain Saturday afternoon, which I well recall, I went mad on paper....

There was a boom in wrestling at the time and the papers were full of photographs of contestants, mostly foreigners, and decidedly fleshy ones. It suddenly occurred to me to try to put the spirit of wrestling into a drawing without bothering a scrap about the correctness of how it was done, and as I worked I felt myself to be exactly as I imagined a wrestler must feel as he faces his opponent and seeks for an opening. It was simply a pair of heavy practically naked men, a Japanese and a Russian, facing one another on a big mat....

I was encouraged to try more along these lines and did so with energy, revelling in this new and powerful mode of expressing an idea that was dependent not upon a joke underneath it, but upon the sheer spirit of the drawing itself. It didn't seem to matter what the subject was, I had only to draw it in this way of getting inside, as it were, and feeling like it. I had really found my true métier and, what was equally gratifying, these things began to attract a lot of notice.

THE SKETCH.

THE SPORT THE BRITISH PUBLIC WILL ATTEND.

"THE ENGLISH ARE A SPORTING NATION!"

It was no coincidence that 'The English are a Sporting Nation!' – by no means one of his best cartoons – is immediately preceded in the chronology of his work by the cartoons on modern drama, but he never seems to have made the connection himself. The relationship between his work and the theatre was further reinforced when he later worked as a theatre artist for *The Sketch* and *The Bystander*, though it was by no means only stage theatre that engaged his attention. All aspects of entertainment and performance interested him, even those he saw outside the theatre. In his descriptions of suburban and middle-class society he was to explore

A SAND-DANCER
from sketch-book.

LITTLE TICH
by Henry Ospovat.

LITTLE TICH
by H. M. Bateman.

that boundary between performance and reality which could be described as 'playing the part' or 'playing the game': he was intrigued by the way in which ordinary people aspire to certain roles, and how enactment of those roles betrays their presumption.

The basis for these observations was not so philosophical but came down to a real delight in the great variety of forms and expressions which performers of all types had naturally to adopt. He never stopped short at mere observation and recording, but always, as with boxing, involved himself as far as possible in the processes he observed. He was, for example, a great amateur of tap-dancing: enthralled by the rhythm and movement of the dancers he saw at the music halls, he set out to buy himself the necessary paraphernalia, shoes and a board, and practised incessantly, shut in a small room at the top of his parents' house, until he had mastered the art. Then, having inveigled his sister into accompanying him on the piano, he would entertain his family and friends with his new skill. It got to the point where he was giving public performances, and nearly decided to give up his career as a cartoonist to go on the stage. This was extraordinary in view of the general description of him as a quiet and intensely shy person, but he always did like applause, and enjoyed nothing more than actually seeing people laughing at his work. He often felt cut off from his audience, working as he did through the impersonality of the magazines.

His hobby did not always inspire affection. Just after the Great War he had a studio in Chelsea, in the same house as, and directly above, A. J. Munnings. Munnings remembered how 'each morning as I worked I could hear H. M. Bateman in the studio above doing his step-dance; pit-a-pat, pit-a-pat, it went on. "Oh damn the fellow!" said I.'[3]

Had Munnings wished to improve his knowledge of the 'step-dance' he would unhesitatingly have gone to the music halls or variety houses, where he could have seen not only dancers of all sorts but an 'extravagant jumble of acrobats, jugglers, conjurers, singers, comics of all kinds.'[4] Bateman was devoted to this type of entertainment, and to the early cinema shows: he was a great fan of Charlie Chaplin, and kept a signed, framed photograph of him. These theatre palaces were as ornate and splendid as their names: the Alhambra, the Tivoli, the Palace, the Gaiety. Bateman drew caricatures of many of the most famous stars – Marie Lloyd, Little Tich, Harry Tate, and Grock the Clown – and his early sketch-books were filled with acrobats and clowns, cross-talkers and cake-walkers, 'singing coons' and chorus girls.

It is perhaps to the music halls and its comedians that he owes something of his slightly surreal humour, at times more peculiar than funny. Many of his cartoons have a 'racy, vital quality'[5] that seems to come straight from them.

In his caricatures of music hall stars, Bateman sometimes adopted a style very much influenced by Henry Ospovat, who died tragically young, aged thirty-one, in 1908.[6] Ospovat had caricatured many of the same performers Bateman was to portray, and his style fascinated Bateman, who tried it out on numerous occasions, though usually for theatrical subjects. He could imitate it almost perfectly, and that he should have wanted to pays tribute to a much-overlooked artist.

Left:
'ALL THIS FOR 3D, 6D AND 1/–'
1911.

In his book *The Edwardians*, J. B. Priestley described just the performers both Bateman and Ospovat were most attracted to.

I was not very fond of the so-called 'eccentric comedians' who came rushing on, in the wierdest costumes, and bawled out nonsensical ditties. There was about them too strong a suggestion of lunacy; and indeed two of the most popular eccentrics committed suicide. But I doted on the great drolls, no matter if they gave solo performances like Little Tich, who contrived somehow to combine furious energy with a certain detachment; or if they had a partner, like the wonderful Grock, who seemed like a serious but bewildered being from another planet; or if they surrounded themselves with infuriatingly daft creatures, like the perpetually amazed and indignant Harry Tate, always the self-important sportsman in a world drifting away from sense and logic, cause and effect. Sketches like Tate's, feasts of unreason, were always arriving in the Edwardian music hall, offering us, to our joy, off-beat, surrealist and even *black* humour sixty years ago.

'TYPES OF THE HALLS.'

One of the cartoons the artist particularly remembered in old age as being a favourite.

Above and Above Right:
THE BYSTANDER
c. 1911.

LONDON OPINION,
c. 1911.

'AN EMINENT ECCLESIASTIC.'

'AN IRATE PARENT.'

'A GUARDIAN OF THE PROPRIETIES.'
Types from the series
'PEOPLE I HAVE NEVER MET.'

Bateman's visits to the halls led, among other things, to a short series, 'Types of the Halls,' for *London Opinion*, at the beginning of 1909. They were very small, very simple drawings, but they were extremely popular, and he quickly followed up with another series during May of the same year. This was a gallery of some thirty-five characters, called 'People I Have Never Met,' and included 'An Eminent Ecclesiastic,' 'An Irate Parent,' and 'A Guardian of the Proprieties.' Though the perception was similar, the treatment was very different to his 'Seaside Types,' which were full-page, tonal cartoons. These were single-figure line drawings – and the beginning of a whole new and rather separate area of Bateman's work: one which some have seen as his most fruitful.

There is an important difference, also, between the 'Types of the Halls' and 'People I Have Never Met': in the later series, later by only a couple of months, he started to use that elegant, long, rhythmic line which was really the hallmark of his great pre-war drawings. It was at once very Edwardian and very much his own, and he controlled it so effectively that, no matter how distorted or deformed his characters became, they were, by its virtue, always beautiful.

This rhythmic line was most obviously developed in his cartoons on music and dancing. They were really part and parcel of his involvement with performers, and his own enthusiasm for dancing particularly. The expressiveness of singers and musicians, the way in which their faces grimace and their bodies contort as they perform, was a key to Bateman's own very physical understanding of emotion. The movement and gracefulness of dance helped him to develop those very qualities in his drawings. He produced many cartoons of musicians – especially piano players – and of singers, dancers and skaters, most of them appearing in *The Sketch*, *The Bystander* and *London Opinion*.

There was now 'hardly a paper published in London which contained a humorous section' to which Bateman did not contribute. He was also beginning to 'live thoroughly.' He took up golf (see chapter 11), and learnt how to fly-fish, through H. T. Sheringham, angling editor of *The Field* – both pastimes providing a great deal of material for his work as well as much enjoyment. He had met Sheringham through his younger brother, George, who became a close friend. George Sheringham was a theatrical designer and illustrator, who had studied at the Slade during the time of Ricketts and Shannon, and was making a name for himself through exhibitions in London and Paris, and sets for the West End stage.[7] Another friend, Frank Hart,[8] black-and-white illustrator, and regular contributor to *Punch* during the 1920s, also came into his life at this time, and was to remain close to Bateman and his family until his death in 1959.

Bateman was then, through his work, being drawn more and more into the company of professional artists: the coterie of cartoonists and illustrators which centred professionally upon the London magazines and socially upon the arts clubs. These clubs, especially the London Sketch Club and the Chelsea Arts Club, meant a great deal to Bateman as to his contemporaries. They provided him, still living at home with his family, with somewhere to exchange ideas, to relax, and to meet other artists, who could stimulate his interest and imagination.

5
THE ARTS CLUBS

The Edwardian age was the golden age of the club, and the London Sketch Club and Chelsea Arts Club were only two of a group of clubs, of which the Langham and the Savage were also a part. Often artists would be members of two or three clubs, and many of Bateman's acquaintances belonged, as he did, to both the Chelsea Arts and the London Sketch Club.

Bateman joined the Sketch Club first, in 1907, and in the signatures book he shares a page with Heath Robinson, Tony Sarg, George Studdy, Harry Rountree, John Hassall and A.R. Thompson. The club was an offshoot of the Langham, and was founded in 1898 when a group of young artists, led by Dudley Hardy and Cecil Aldin, decided that the older institution was proving a little too stuffy.[1] Though its gatherings were light-hearted and often rather raucous, there had been from its inauguration a serious central idea to the weekly meetings: each member had to complete a two-hour sketch 'from seven till nine, the subjects being chosen by committees at the beginning of the year, one for figure, another for landscape'.[2] Afterwards, the work would be put on display, for criticism by members and guests. Membership was not merely by election, as was the case with the Chelsea Arts, but work had to be submitted to the committee for examination. At the end of each year an exhibition was organized, to which the general public was invited, and which was frequently and often enthusiastically reviewed in the Press.[3]

So the Sketch Club, while it maintained the character of an exclusive Edwardian social club, was very much a dynamic society of working artists, who took pleasure not only in each other's company but also in each other's work. In his book on the club, David Cuppleditch shows how often groups or pairs of artists admired and inspired one another. There was, among the black-and-white artists, almost a sense of a Sketch Club style – or perhaps two or three styles – which becomes apparent in the pages of such papers as *The Sketch* (no direct connection with the club) or *The Bystander*.

Though there were some resemblances between Bateman's work and that of his fellows – especially, at this time, Frank Reynolds – Bateman was something of an exception to this rule, being, by temperament and commitment, very much the individualist. Though an enthusiast, he was also shy and introspective, and while he entered into activities which involved his own personal commitment to some particular skill or practice, he was never outgoing enough to participate strongly in group activity. He seems to have taken up what became a customary position, slightly on the edge of things – the observer – and never held a central role within the club, although he was most regular in his attendance. The club's history is

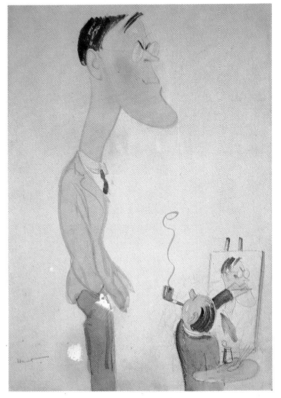

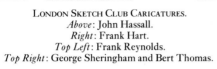

LONDON SKETCH CLUB CARICATURES.
Above: John Hassall.
Right: Frank Hart.
Top Left: Frank Reynolds.
Top Right: George Sheringham and Bert Thomas.

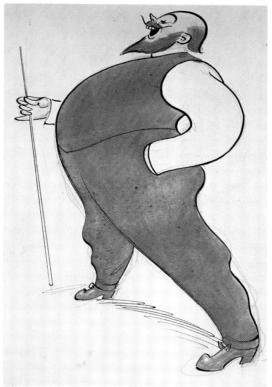

filled with amusing anecdotes, but he did not take much part in the buffoonery, being much happier to sit aside and draw caricatures of other members. These were generally applauded with great fervour, except by the individual involved, who would take him to one side, muttering, 'But you know, Bateman, you've missed me. I am not like that.'[4]

The best descriptions of the club come from Bateman himself, as he remembered it in his old age.

CHELSEA ARTS CLUB CARICATURES.
Above: George Lambert.
Above Left: A. E. Johnson
(Bateman's agent) and Gilmer.

The London Sketch Club existed for work and entertainment, and I must begin with a description of its premises as, without doubt, these were the foundation on which the active spirit and success of the club rested.

For the purpose the premises were ideal. They were situated in Wells Street, off Oxford Street, and consisted simply of a huge top-floor room, or garret, complete with ancient beams and a chimney corner of the old sort, all redolent of Bohemia. It was reached from the street by a steep enclosed wooden staircase, so narrow that two persons could barely pass on it.

We had a small bar, where beer in solid stone mugs and a few aperitifs were supplied, and we had a small stage about ten feet square centrally placed for short performances. A remarkable feature was a frieze of silhouette portraits, all life-size, of every member, which ran just below the ceiling, right around the room. I remember sitting for my silhouette in the small darkened office, with a lamp to throw my shadow, when the member responsible for making them operated on

THE FRIEZE
from the walls of the
London Sketch Club.

me soon after my election. I did not obtain election on my first attempt – when I submitted a highly-wrought oil painting it smacked rather too much of the art student, I believe – however I tried again a bit later with something more imaginative, which succeeded, and I was duly admitted into the fold. I was then the youngest member of the club, a distinction I enjoyed for a number of years until another youngster arrived on the scene to oust me from that position.

THE LONDON SKETCH CLUB.
Bateman is indicated by
an arrow.

The black-and-white men, prominent illustrators and humorists of those days, were, in point of numbers, the biggest section. Among them were: Tom Browne; Lawson Wood; Starr Wood; John Hassall; Renee Bull; Frank Reynolds; Frank Hart; Lance Thackeray; Bert Thomas; Heath Robinson; and there were some notable serious artists with: George Sheringham; Hughes Stanton; Edmund Dulac; Charles Dixon – a marine painter; Geoffrey Strahan – a most promising young painter, alas killed in Gallipoli; Dudley Hardy, so versatile; Joseph Harker, the scene painter who was responsible for much scenery in

Beerbohm Tree's stage productions. Colonel Baden-Powell, the hero of Mafeking and founder of the Boy Scouts was, I believe, a member or honorary member, at any rate he appeared there on occasions. Baden-Powell was uncommonly good at pencil drawing . . .

We met on Friday evenings . . . and two titles were given. We worked for two hours on whichever subject we liked, and then put our work on show for discussion and criticism. Needless to say the variety of interpretations of the same title were often extraordinary. By this time the lay members began to arrive and joined in the general review – they were not expected to show up during the working period – and the long table was being laid for supper of the boiled beef and carrots order, though roast joints were frequent, and an occasional steak and kidney pudding evening was something of an event.

After supper an impromptu smoking concert followed, and that could go on till the early hours of the next morning if there was enough talent on hand. Many of the lay members were professional entertainers of one sort and another; singers, musicians, reciters – all very skilled and generous in their readiness to do a turn. And many famous figures in the entertainment world, when performing in London, were brought along by somebody who knew them. It was almost the thing to do to visit the London Sketch Club and do a short turn there.

When the winter ended we had a full-scale exhibition – the only time when ladies were admitted to this all-male stronghold. It came to an end when the lease on the place ran out and could not be renewed. The club moved into smaller quarters in the Marylebone Road and did its best to carry on there. But something was lacking, some of the old vitality had gone, and we put it down to the loss of that atmosphere which had prevailed in our unique Wells Street top floor.[5]

The move to Marylebone took place in 1913, but before this, while the Sketch Club was still in full swing, Bateman was proposed by Frank Hart for election to the Chelsea Arts Club, and was admitted on August 5, 1910. Unlike the Sketch Club, which only opened one evening a week, the Chelsea Arts Club was open all the time, and even, after the War, provided beds for those of its members who wished to stay overnight. It was a place to sit and drink and talk, and it became almost a second home to Bateman, especially during the War years, when he was particularly disorientated. He described it as 'a madhouse which paradoxically kept us sane.' It was his sanctuary when on the run from the outside world. He remained closely attached to it until his marriage, in 1926, often giving it as his address, and only resigned his membership in old age, and with regret, in 1958.

What made the club so attractive, beside its availability and easy-going ambience, was undoubtedly its membership. It was a far larger establishment than the Sketch Club, and had a broader base, the black-and-white men being here in the minority. Because there was a constant stream of people rushing in and out, on their way to and from other

THE HISTORY OF THE CHELSEA ARTS CLUB

BY THE
HON. SEC. GRAHAM PETRIE

Illustrated by H. M. BATEMAN

" The Six Bells was at that time a charming old-fashioned pub "

THE origin of the Club was a very elemental and prosaic one—the need of wholesome food. For in 1889—the date of its inception—Chelsea, though no longer the rural village beloved by Sir Thomas More, Queen Catherine of Braganza and Nell Gwynne, was still unsophisticated according to the standards of to-day. Locomotion was dependent on hansom cabs, which few could afford, or slow horse buses, and thus we were

" Relaxation for our minds "

obliged, in the main, to put up with the local resources :

The Six Bells was at that time a charming, old-fashioned country pub, with a perfect bowling-green, but it confined its sale of solid food to " sausages and mash " plus ham sandwiches, and there was but one restaurant within easy reach, a dangerously bad one.

So to banish fear of premature death by misadventure, it was proposed to form a purely Dining Club, and to this end terms were actually discussed with the firm of Spiers and Pond.

But the mention of the magic word " Club " will always arouse in optimistic minds—and no artist could exist unless an optimist—fantastic visions of an Earthly Paradise.

Do not let us pretend, we argued, that our needs are confined to food for the body. We also require stimulants for our nerves at odd moments, relaxation for our minds, diversions for our wits and a host of other things.

We require a real Club, an artist's club, a unique club, such a club as will put to shame dull conventional clubs, organised by Philistines.

And so the Chelsea Arts Club was born. It is now the oldest and largest club in England where membership is confined to those practising the graphic and plastic arts.

" We also require stimulants "

The venture was, from the first, a great success, and the writer has vivid memories of gay buoyant hours passed in the rather stuffy and confined atmosphere of our first clubhouse which stood on the site of the present Chenil Galleries.

Conspicuous among our Foundation

" Diversions for our wits "

engagements, there was an atmosphere of excitement, of things happening and being done. Most of the famous painters of the time were there: Augustus John, Walter Sickert, Wilson Steer, Orpen, Tonks, Munnings, Albert Toft, and Hughes Stanton. Arthur Rackham and Edmund Dulac were both members, and another illustrator and painter, Philip Connard, who taught at the Lambeth School of Art, became one of Bateman's closer friends at the club. Again Bateman drew many caricatures of the members, and some are still to be seen on the walls today. He also designed the décor for the Chelsea Arts Ball on at least one occasion.

The club's historian, T. H. H. Hancock, is cautious of claiming any great seminal role for it: 'I do not really believe,' he wrote, 'that the club has ever really influenced the work of any artist.'[6] But there were

---

Members was Whistler, always quivering with restless vitality, kind-hearted, yet loving to watch his darts of wit impart a harmless sting. And John Sargent, who presented us with an excellent piano, a

" George Lambert and Philip Connard "

good trencherman, one worthy of the village of Henry VIII, who always ordered a steak for lunch in addition to the Club menu.

Of those who were in at the start, or joined us a little later, and have since won their laurels, and made their names household words, I may mention: Walter Sickert, John Lavery, Will Llewellyn, Frank Short, Augustus John, Wilson Steer, Will Orpen, Derwent Wood, Pomeroy, Havard Thomas, George Henry, J. J. Shannon, George Clausen, George Lambert, Philip Connard,

" Our garden with its velvety bowling green "

Adrian Jones and Terrick Williams — though there are many others of equal distinction.

In 1901 our lease came to an end and we were glad to move to our present home in Church Street — a cottage, when we took it, with small rooms and low ceilings, yet homely and cosy — a remnant of Chelsea

village. Addition had to be made, but happily much of the old-world flavour remains.

And we love our garden with its velvety bowling green, its pergola, and its gay flower beds. When the trees are in full foliage hardly a hint of bricks and mortar can be discerned, and we like to fancy that the ghosts of Nell Gwynne and her gay Monarch join in our merriment when from time to time we welcome our lady friends to a fête champêtre.

It was in 1907 that some-one asked this pertinent question: "Why is it that while in other great cities, Paris, Munich, Rome, etc., balls and pageants, organised by artists, have achieved world-wide fame, the artists of London have rarely enlivened their capital by such charming revels?" Were we lacking, it was asked, in the needful wit, fancy and daring; or did we scowl, like grim Puritans, at the spirit of fun and frolic?

"Augustus John"

" Did we scowl like grim Puritans ?"

The jibe rankled, and we resolved to prove to the world that the art of pageantry and the love of jollity were not dead in London Town.

But the romance of the Chelsea Arts Club Balls will be told on another page by our Chairman, George Sherwood Foster.

" The ghosts of Nell Gwynne and her gay Monarch "

obviously opportunities for artists to discuss their work, and undoubtedly such preoccupations were allowed to intrude occasionally into the pleasurable round of the club's activities. There is no record of Wilson Steer ever making creatively provocative remarks to Walter Sickert, or of Augustus John giving A. J. Munnings tips on the anatomy of the horse, but there is evidence that between Bateman and his circle of friends there were some helpful interchanges. Among portfolios in the club's possession there is a collection of caricature portraits by Bateman, A. R. Thomson, Bert Thomas and others, which show similarities. Though they were all no doubt descended from the same stable – the *portraits chargés* of Beerbohm and Pelligrini – and also, in Bateman's case, from those early family and schoolboy caricatures which appear in his sketch-books, such caricatures seem to have become a kind of competitive in-joke at this club. Just as Bateman was encouraged to draw such caricatures in the London Sketch Club, where, with a strong contingent of humorous artists, there was already a lively tradition of caricature well established, so he seems to have helped encourage a similar tradition at the Chelsea Arts Club.

Undoubtedly, though, talk was the glue which held the club together, and Bateman loved to listen to the great talkers, like Derwent Wood and George Lambert. The character of the conversation was generally friendly, but occasionally discussions became rather heated, and it was felt expedient to help maintain a certain level of decorum by writing into the club's constitution a rule against violent behaviour and loose language. A. J. Munnings, though later reinstated, was in fact expelled for using bad language, and there were a number of incidents, recorded in the council minute books, which aroused some concern. In 1911, there was a complaint made against a member who had called another 'a rascal,' and said, 'I have a d.....d mind (siezing him by the arm) to knock your bloody eyes out and wring your bloody neck, you d.....d little rat.' Such eloquence and diplomacy was only matched by the secretary's letter to the offending member. 'I am to invite your attention to no. XXVIII of the Club Rules, and to request that you will favour me with an explanation in accordance with the provisions of that rule.'[7] There were many such infringements of Rule 28.

No official history of the club has been published, but not long after he joined, Bateman provided some little sketches for a brief account of its evolution, written by the secretary, Graham Petrie, and published in *The Bystander*.

In 1911 Bateman had his first exhibition. It took place at the Brook Street Gallery, and the work consisted mostly of his caricatures of members of the Chelsea Arts Club and the London Sketch Club, and of theatrical personalities. It was described as 'the most amusing thing that has been seen in London this season,' and was, as the writer in *London Opinion* remarked, 'an achievement indeed for an artist in his twenty-fourth year.'[8] It set the seal on Bateman's reputation, but it was really only concerned with one part of his work: the humorous portraits. Though some of his 'Rinking Types' and 'People I Have Never Met' were also shown, there were none of his newest cartoons, his very funny but often rather acid observations on society and the polite middle-class world which he and his family inhabited in the suburban heartland of Clapham.

6
LIFE IN THE SUBURBS

The first collection of Bateman's cartoons, published in 1916, was called *Burlesques*, the third, published in 1921, *Suburbia*, and together the titles say much about his approach and his chosen material. For some time, in his drawings of people at fairs and at the seaside, he had commented on certain kinds of social behaviour with a humorous though mocking irony. Although his characters were comic, they were viewed with a certain affection. Some time after his breakdown, perhaps merely because he was losing some of his youthful innocence, the element of ridicule in his cartoons became more marked: an aspect of his work which was to deepen considerably as time went on. Indeed, he gained a reputation as a precocious cynic: something he did not really deserve, for his cartoons at this time were not savagely satirical. As A. E. Johnson, his agent, wrote in the Introduction to *Burlesques*, 'the satirist seeks to impose satirical exaggeration upon a situation not necessarily of itself humorous, whereas Bateman tries to reveal humour not impose it.'

'THE REMOVAL MAN'
from 'Children of Toil'.

He was also considered a purveyor of the grotesque, yet although he did find certain extremes of form and behaviour rather attractive, it was by no means only the oddity of the odd with which he dealt, but the oddity of the ordinary person: in this lay the burlesque. And to Bateman the ordinary person was largely suburban man. After all, he was himself suburban, and he merely used the material closest at hand. He could spy out the land with an already intimate knowledge of its inhabitants, and an understanding of every nuance, every raised eyebrow. In 1910, his family moved from 2 Bonneville Road, Clapham, to a house a few streets away, Parkstone, 40 Nightingale Lane, which had a large studio room for Bateman, and was in a more 'desirable' position.

In his book on suburbia, published in 1905, T. W. H. Crosland wrote, 'It is fair and reasonable to call Clapham the capital of Suburbia. If you walk down the Clapham Road from the end of the Common to Clapham Road Station, with your eyes open, you will have seen the best part of all that Suburbia has to show.'[1] Crosland also castigated suburban life, writing that, in Clapham, 'you will perceive that whizzers, penny buses, gramophones, bamboo furniture, pleasant Sunday afternoons, glossy songs, modern language teas, golf, tennis, higher education, dubious fiction, shilling worth of comic writing, picture postcards, miraculous hair restorers, prize competitions, and all the other sorts of twentieth-century claptrap, have got a market and a use and black masses of supporters.' There is a Victorian snobbery here. What was wrong with whizzers? The real problem with suburbia was that through topographical separation the suburbans inhabited a world of their own, with little contact outside their own class, and with other values. From 1901 there were electric trams in London – an electric tube line had been established some years before – and a generally greater mobility allowed those who could afford it to escape the clutter of the city and migrate to the tidy rows of villas that had sprung up in Clapham, Hampstead, and other outlying areas.[2] The suburbans grasped gentility with fervour, and, like the Bateman family, rejected the numbers on their gateposts, calling their houses by names – a fashion which *Punch* had pilloried in 1904. There was a sudden flurry of Bellevues, Moss Denes, Granges and Crofts.

Of course, the reason for the *Punch* satires and Crosland's book was the newness of suburbia. A sudden and fundamental change had occurred in the city's way of life, blurring the traditional division between the town and the country. All through the Edwardian era, town centres were becoming depopulated, the middle classes seizing the opportunity to move into what had until recently been countryside. In his *History of England*, A. J. P. Taylor wrote of this period that 'All England became suburban except the slums at one extreme and the Pennine Moors at the other.'[3] An exaggeration perhaps, but the sensation that a new species had just arisen, or descended, was real enough.

No cartoonist was to chronicle this new species so consistently or successfully as Bateman. Between 1909 and 1914, hardly a week passed without some other passion of suburban man anatomized in *London Opinion*, *The Sketch* or *The Bystander*. Years before, John Hassall had noticed this tendency in Bateman to base his cartoon characters on personalities he saw around his home – and dubbed him the 'Suburban Artist.'

'COMING OF AGE',
from the series 'Outside
the Four-Mile Radius:
Suburbia'.

Opposite:
THE DOGS.
QUITE FRIENDLY, IT IS TRUE,
BUT TOO UNPLEASANTLY ANXIOUS
TO LICK YOUR FACE.'
From the series
'Social Terrors'.

Outside the Four-Mile Radius: Suburbia.

III.—AT HOME DAY.

It will be recalled that, a while ago, we decided to discontinue for a time Mr. Bateman's Suburbia Series, that we might publish his Winter-Sports Series in proper season. We now restart the set which began in our issue of Jan. 31 last.

DRAWN BY H. M. BATEMAN.

Among Bateman's funniest and most apposite cartoons in this field were those that described the social round of visits paid and received, entertainments and distractions pursued, and parties given. During July 1910, his series 'Social Terrors' began to appear in *London Opinion*. The cartoons centred around the idea of a guest trapped by an enthusiasm he did not share: mother making the children play duets for him, or being forced to look through endless family photo albums. One of the best is 'The Dogs.'

The situations remain entirely recognizable. Another series, published in *The Sketch*, was 'Outside the Four-Mile Radius: Suburbia.' (Anything that was obviously connected to London but was more than four miles from the centre was called suburbia.) The young man suffering torments as the object of paternal pride, the chattering ladies at tea, the hidden conflicts within the church parade – all speak eloquently of the customs and behaviour of an aspiring class.

The aspiration, or emulation, of these characters lay in their attempts to mirror the behaviour of their social 'superiors.' They were, of course, deeply conservative. Not necessarily because they identified with the policies of the Conservative Party, but because that party was supposed to be the one favoured by the wealthy and fashionable classes.[4] They therefore acquired many of the appurtenances of the fashionable and wealthy – but never quite their style. During Edwardian times there was a fiercely competitive struggle up the ladder of what has been called the 'shopocracy,' and it was this competitive element, based on money made from business rather than inherited wealth, which lent such piquancy to their social relations. Writers of the time, like Wells in *Tono Bungay*, refer to the '*nouveau riche*' or the '*parvenu*' in the most disparaging terms – though often not as disparaging as the comments of the established aristocracy, indignant that money was usurping breeding, yet more than eager to take the cash if it came their way. They strongly resented the friendship of King Edward with men like Sir Thomas Lipton, the founder of what are now the Lipton supermarkets, saying that he had taken up with his grocer.

In July and August 1910, *The Bystander* published a series of six Bateman cartoons on 'The Parvenu's Progress' which illustrated the pitfalls of such social mobility. Many of the scenes have an almost tangible atmosphere of discomfort. Bateman, of course, was not the first or only artist to mock the social climber or parvenu. Du Maurier, for example, created two famous beings, Sir George Midas and Mrs Ponsonby Tompkins, who became much loved by readers of *Punch*.

Social display revealed much of the folly of the new breed. They liked to puff themselves up, and show off their feathers, and it was in the drawing-room or out in the street after church on Sunday that they took the opportunity to do so. It has been said that the middle classes only went to church because they thought it important to set an example to the lower classes – who were probably miles away – but it was also important that everyone should show exactly what they thought of themselves and everybody else. The church parade was an occasion which called forth all the resources of the wardrobe, and the whole vocabulary of glance and gesture.

From 'Children of Toil'.

'THE SWEEP.'

'THE CHARWOMAN.'

APRIL 17, 1912   THE SKETCH.   55

Outside the Four - Mile Radius : Suburbia.

IV.   CHURCH PARADE.
Drawn by H. M. Bateman.

'CROYDON: THE GARDEN',
from 'Life in Our Suburbs'.

> The Church Parade beats everything,
> The Church Parade when in full swing
> Is a thing to see and wonder at
> For Oh, the wealth displayed
> Of the millinery art,
> And costumes smart
> In the Church Parade.[5]

The vicar must have sat rather uneasily among his flock so well-groomed and bristling. On the other hand, perhaps he felt no incongruity, for he was himself part of the social scene, gracing many a tea-time gathering with his avuncular presence. Men of the cloth had almost a free pass into

The Parvenu's Progress

Left:
THE BYSTANDER,
17 August 1910.

From 'Life in Our Suburbs'.

'TOOTING.'

'BROMLEY TO KESTON
AND BACK.'

5. HIS DAUGHTER CONSENTS TO RESTORE THE FORTUNES OF A NOBLE RACE

feminine society, and did much to raise the pulses of the million so-called 'redundant women' of Edwardian times. They were overtly asexual repositories for confidences and tittle-tattle, while covertly, of course, quite the opposite. It was a charade. Bateman delighted in vicars, drawing them over and over again in all shapes and sizes and attitudes of body and mind. To a black-and-white artist they offered wonderful scope: white collars and black clothes the basic format upon which to work. Bateman even created his own kind of holy folk hero, Prebendary Orpington, who, transformed to suit each situation, is his celebration of the wonderful eccentricity of the breed.

In these cartoons, beautifully and rhythmically drawn in ink, many with a colour wash, Bateman makes a speciality of coy delight, eliciting the

'NOW CHILDREN. EPPING.'
From 'Life in Our Suburbs'.

'THE TEA PARTY.'

peculiar charm of living in a sexually repressed society. His characters are charged with an inner ecstasy, and again, despite the freedom and exaggeration of form, everything is understated. In 'The Tea Party,' for instance, the tea cups and the canary above do as much to create the atmosphere as the lovely ugliness of the three celebrants. It is a fine example of Bateman practising the precepts of his favourite and probably only quotation from Aristotle: 'The aim of art is to represent not the outward appearance of things but their inward significance.'

The female counterparts of Bateman's vicars were his maiden aunts. In the cartoon 'The Evil Eye – Chaperones,' their watchful and disapproving presence not only describes their own social role but also the scene before them. The cartoon leaves much to the imagination, gaining some of its effect by what it leaves out, and some by the few stage props

'HE COMETH!'
London Opinion,
13 January 1912.

'THE ATHLETE',
from 'Sporting Types'.

assembled to help the description. The lorgnettes, the fans, the discarded dance-book, the bottle of smelling salts, the ostrich plume, are emblems of that Victorian legacy which the unseen dancers reject, along with the rigidity of manner and costume assumed by their chaperones. Edwardian gossip held that those austere dresses with the high necks were made fashionable by Queen Alexandra, who wanted to hide the scars resulting from her husband's more unfortunate liaisons. A wicked thought neither Bateman nor his maiden aunts would have countenanced.

It was perhaps when Bateman tracked down his contemporaries finally at rest around the meal table that he became most eloquent: the poet of food and drink. The Edwardians seem to have had a particularly self-indulgent approach to the problems of nourishment. Donald Read, in his book *Edwardian England*, wrote that 'Elaborate over-eating was one of the

LONDON

ONE PENNY.

18th MAY. 1912.

Vol. XXXIII. No. 426.

(Reg. G.P.O.)

OPINION

| EXCLUSIVE NEWS ROUND THE TOWN. | THIS PUBLICATION CARRIES A FREE INSURANCE OF £2000. UNDERTAKEN BY THE OCEAN ACCIDENT & GUARANTEE CORPORATION, LTD. | MANY DRAWINGS BY FAMOUS ARTISTS. |

Cartoons from 'In the Trade'.

'THE WATCH MAKER.'

THE TOWN MOUSE AND THE COUNTRY MOUSE.

L.O. SUMMER ANNUAL WILL BE ON SALE ON MONDAY.

'THE TAILOR.'

'THE SWEET S

THE FIRST LESSON.

'THE COBBLER.'

PLATONIC LOVE.

Drawn by H. M. Bateman.

'THE FLORIST',
also from 'In the Trade'.

'THE EVIL EYE – CHAPERONES.'

most noticeable Edwardian vices, extending from the aristocracy and plutocracy well down into the middle class.' Most noticeable perhaps not so much because a sudden delight in over-eating seized the population but that, with the proliferation of restaurants, respectable people could now indulge their appetites in public. At the least elaborate level this could be seen in the rise of the tea-room, the Aerated Bread Company tea shops, and Lyons Corner House – new Edwardian concerns where now, for the first time, women as well as men could sit and eat their midday meal unaccompanied.[6] They catered for the new working woman, the telephonist, and secretary, whose numbers until now had been small – they had previously taken packed lunches, for public houses were, of course, out of the question – and for the middle-class clerk, who wished to

'AUNTS.'

Cartoons from 'Nourishment'.

'STOUT AND OYSTERS.'

'CUTLETS AND CLARET.'

'ASPARAGUS IS NOW IN SEASON.' *London Opinion*, 22 May 1909.

'MIXED VERMOUTH.'

'GRENADINE.'

'SARDINES ON TOAST.'

disassociate himself from the packed lunch and its working-class connotations, and who lived too far away, in suburbia, to return home for his midday meal.

Though these were new eating habits, and Bateman recorded them, he was more attracted by the pleasure-seeker than the convenience eater. He was himself an abstinent man, hardly touching alcohol, and eating only what he needed, but he did describe the habits of his friends and acquaintances, and one can imagine him at a dinner party, satisfied but not dulled, sitting back to watch them. The man who was to become Bateman's greatest friend, William Caine, produced a little comic masterpiece, called *The Glutton's Mirror*, in which he wrote, 'I say roundly that humanity gets its greatest pleasure out of its victuals.'[7] Caine was a glutton of impeccable taste, and gives real insight into the philosophy of the seven-course meal.

The friendship between the two men started in 1912, and they often dined together. Despite being able to put away a large quantity of food, Caine was witty and erudite, knowledgeable and sensitive about what he ate. He utterly condemned the English sauce, and warned against the larger indecencies of the table. 'Some people roast their hare whole and carve it at the table before your eyes. This should not be allowed. A trussed bird looks less like a bird than anything one can imagine, but a roasted hare looks more like a baby than anything one can have nightmares about.'[8]

Bateman occasionally drew pictures of gross feeders – inventing a huge couple called the Goblets, most frequently to be seen at an overladen table with some cadaverous waiter in the background – but he did not display that repulsed sensitivity to over-eating and its effects on the figure characteristic of a Gillray or Rowlandson. His cartoons were, of course, much less ribald, but he seems to have genuinely enjoyed the spectacle of man at table.

When Edwardians wanted to have a really good time, they ate twice in one evening – dinner before a show, and supper after it – so there was more than usual scope for Bateman to observe them at his and their leisure. However, much of his best work, while based on observation, is more purely imaginative: compositions upon the theme of the secret empathy between eater and eaten. Outstanding at this period were his simple, beautifully drawn pen sketches, his series of 'Types,' among which he produced, between 1911 and 1912, a set of eaters and drinkers under the general heading of 'Nourishment.' In his book *Comic Art in England*, Cornelius Veth wrote that to see Bateman's 'really great graphic humour at its best,' one should look at 'the gentleman who takes stout and oysters, and the other who prefers whisky and soda, the woman drinking juniper berry, and the old lady drinking tea, the particular ladies to whom sardines on toast, or it may be cutlets and claret, are the greatest delicacy.'[9]

As well as the series 'Nourishment' there appeared, between 1910 and 1912, 'Children of Toil,' 'In the Trade,' 'Sporting Types,' and 'Life in Our Suburbs.' Though one may prefer other of his creations, these little drawings are special and perfect, combining his best qualities of humorous understanding with an immaculate and graceful graphic skill. The inspiration for them lay in the streets and shops around Bateman's home. Yet at the same time he was using material not so close at hand.

7
SOME POLITICS

Bateman has been sometimes criticized for having let the great political events of the twentieth century roll past him unnoticed – for having lived in a kind of P. G. Wodehouse wonderland. Such criticism, though uninformed, implies that a good cartoonist ought to have a serious moral and especially political intent, that he should be committed to some particular view of the world, and should use his skill to influence and disturb. David Low, for example, one of the greatest political cartoonists, and a deeply committed artist in every sense, annoyed Hitler to such an extent that he was put on the Führer's notorious black list – a list of nuisances to be eliminated upon triumphal entry into England. Low used drawing as an offensive weapon. In his book on British cartoonists[1] he discussed with admiration Leech's attacks on Disraeli, which had the great politician so worried that he tried personally to placate the cartoonist. He also told how Leech designed the 'Graham Envelope.'

> Mr Graham, the then Home Secretary, was alleged to have opened some private letters in the exercise of his official privilege. Leech drew a neat design of steaming kettles, Paul Prys, and snakes in the grass, which was printed on envelopes and had an immense sale for use through the post. Mr Graham was effectively cured of his paternalism.

This was what Low admired in a cartoonist, what he set out to do himself, and it particularizes his whole conception of the cartoonist's art. He wrote of Phil May, whom he greatly admired as a draughtsman and humorous artist, that he 'was not a good cartoonist, for he had no political sense and his drawings hardly ever had an objective moral.'[2]

This strong line held by Low finds a dilute corollary in criticisms upon Bateman and others who did not concern themselves with the major political dramas of the day. It is a very limited historical perspective which decides that these dramas are of any greater significance than the life of the individual, for attention which is paid to political events and which focusses on the outward forms of the struggle – the politicians involved, the statements made – may well miss the main significance of such events. Since it was people and not ideas that interested Bateman, it is churlish to demand an ideological treatment merely because it may be in some way intellectually more serious. During these Edwardian years, most people were not terribly interested in intellectual statements – not even political ones – not the people who bought the humorous magazines certainly. They wanted to be amused. Indeed, editorial policy insisted they were. No

"THE LOVE-BIRDS."

A PARLIAMENTARY IDYLL.

It is pleasant to reflect that Mr. Churchill and Mr. Lloyd George are still firm friends, notwithstanding the many vicissitudes through which their somewhat erratically led party has recently passed

SKETCHED IN THE HOUSE OF COMMONS BY H. M. BATEMAN

one had yet imagined that the magazine could provide space for political statements such as Low's.

Bateman in fact did pay some attention to the politics of his day, though he always emphasized the human aspect, and his cartoons do not show any particular leaning, one way or another. He used sometimes to go to the House of Commons and sit in the visitors' gallery. It appealed strongly to his sense of the absurd. He liked the show, and enjoyed debunking the myth of earnest representation the Commons put about. Just as today, it was often silliness and self-interest that characterized its procedures. Equally often it was just plain boring nonsense.

'The Member for Mudhampton Introduces his Bill on the Subject of Crabs' Claws', 1910.

He was quick to illustrate the comic in political debate. In 1911, Lloyd George introduced his Insurance Act, the forebear of National Insurance, which proposed, as *The Sketch* explained beneath Bateman's cartoon, 'that every servant shall be insured by special stamps to be paid for half by the mistress and half by the servant, and stuck on a special card.' The act was in itself utterly reasonable, but Bateman's conviction that people would make nonsense of it was borne out in reality. There was the most extraordinary fuss and bother. The act was greeted by employers as yet another instance of the State interfering with personal liberty, and by the employed as an attempt to rob them of still more money. One Edwardian lady even hired the Albert Hall for a meeting on the subject, and declared that the Act would ruin the 'beautiful and intimate relationship which had hitherto existed between mistress and servant.'[3]

In those days of an emergent welfare system, it worried many people that the State, with its officials, should be allowed to order the individual even in this small respect. The whole question of State versus individual had sprung into life, and eventually it became, for Bateman, one of overriding concern. As he grew older, he treated 'the system' with a growing degree of passion and venom.

Female suffrage was another great issue of the times. Lord Curzon

'THE SOCIALIST.'

made apoplectic speeches declaring that it would bring about the destruction of the Empire, while a more reasonable man like Sir Arthur Conan Doyle believed it would destroy the family unit, and hated the violent behaviour of the suffragettes, which he considered grotesque. Wells and Shaw, both supporters of the movement, came under a good deal of suspicion on account of their ideas on 'free love,' and the whole movement became tied up with socialism and all its concomitant horrors, through its connection with Keir Hardie. The movement's leaders did it considerable harm through their wild behaviour, and even Wells was moved to write that 'It became increasingly evident that a large part of the women's suffrage movement was animated less by the desire for freedom and fullness of life than a passionate jealousy and hatred of the relative liberties of men.'[4] Mrs Pankhurst became so hysterical that she seems to have believed the vote for women would stop their menstruation. The suffragettes held demonstrations at theatres and public meetings, until dragged out fighting. 'It was as though a vicarage tea party had suddenly changed into a witch's Sabbath.'[5]

Here was a real cause for a politically committed cartoonist to set his teeth into. Bateman, though he must have had ideas on the relative justice of the matter, was only concerned to show the travesty which people worked upon themselves, and pointed an ironic finger at the absurdities and incongruities of the movement, and the bewildered reaction of the general public. Now, of course, one remembers that suffragettes were taken down back alleys and beaten up by policemen. At the time, however,

An Emerald Evening in the Commons

Mr. Flurry O'Reilly, M.P. for the Knockballingrath Division of Connemara, rises to say a few words on "th' vile quistion av the co-ercion av th' tinants an the Shreelandounane istate"

BY H. M. BATEMAN

THE STICK-STAMPS ACT: WHAT MAY BE AND MIGHT HAVE BEEN.

MR. LLOYD GEORGE'S IDEA FROM GERMANY: IN THE DAYS OF THE SERVANT TAX. AS IMAGINED
BY OUR ARTIST.

We need scarcely tell our readers that that clause of the Insurance Bill which proposes that every servant shall be insured by means of special stamps, to be paid for half by the mistress and half by the servant, and stuck on a special card, has aroused an extraordinary amount of discussion. The idea, it may be noted, comes from Germany. Some results of the way in which the matter has inspired our Artist are here given. It will be seen that Mr. Bateman has not noticed the Chancellor's denial that it is intended that an inspector may enter a private dwelling-house to see whether the conditions of the Act are being complied with. Thus, he illustrates not only what may be, but what might have been.

DRAWN BY H. M. BATEMAN.

'THE M.P. SEEKS RE-ELECTION', *London Opinion*, 17 December 1910.

Above:
'THE GENERAL PUBLIC.'

Above Right:
'WE WILL HAVE IT.'

perhaps Bateman's attitude was exactly what was needed to deflate the intransigent self-importance, and the violence on both sides.

Of course, in none of this was he a political cartoonist in Low's sense, and though he drew caricatures of many of the political figures of the day – of Churchill and Lloyd George, of John Redmond and Augustine Birrell – it was their personalities rather than their policies that engaged him.

It was perhaps merely an extension of his interest in acting and dramatic behaviour that led him into the Commons in the first place, and in 1912 he decided to devote the greater part of his energies to working as the theatre artist for *The Sketch*, a post which he held for two years, and which both enthralled and exhausted him.

8
At the Theatre:
'Our Untamed
Artist'

After a hundred years of bleakness, the theatre nationally, during the Edwardian age, enjoyed a renaissance at all levels. As with the visual arts, there was a sudden burst of activity around the turn of the century. Harley Granville-Barker's productions of Shakespeare swept away the clutter of the Victorian stage, and writers like Shaw brought a new seriousness, a more modern humour. For the first time, a visual artist of stature, Gordon Craig, applied himself to stage design, and in doing so changed the visual expectations of the audience, and the character of the theatre. One Granville-Barker production Bateman sketched was *A Winter's Tale*, where 'there was much that was truly beautiful and original in the setting – a debt to Mr Gordon Craig, whose influence is clearly discoverable.'[1] Bateman found himself in a changing, new and inventive world on which, over a number of months, he was called upon to comment, often twice or three times a week.

In March and April 1910 he had worked for *The Bystander*, adding his illustrations to the theatrical review page, and the first play he attended in this role was Granville-Barker's *The Madras House*, soon followed by *The Toymaker of Nuremburg*, for which his friend George Sheringham had designed the sets. He was also sent along to the latest revues, which had become very popular, and to variety theatres.

It was not until 1912 that he started to work for *The Sketch* and was billed as 'Our Untamed Artist at the Play.' His work took the same form as it had done in *The Bystander*: small incidental sketches and a full- or half-page treatment of the principal actors, often with some smaller sketches interspersed in the text of the review. In his autobiography he wrote:

In 1912 *The Sketch* asked me to try a weekly series of drawings illustrating their theatre pages, amounting to a full page illustrating the chief points in the production under review, and several smaller sketches to be placed among the letterpress, which was done by E. F. Spence under the pseudonym of 'Monocle.' Spence, who was a barrister by day, was the leading dramatic critic at the time. It turned out to be a great success, although just at first some of the actors were rather annoyed at seeing themselves so violently portrayed . . . but they very quickly came round when the series continued, and before long *The Sketch* had requests from producers on the eve of a 'first night' for

BY OUR UNTAMED ARTIST: "THE YELLOW JACKET."

THE INTENSELY INVISIBLE! MR. HOLMAN CLARK AS THE PROPERTY-MAN, AT THE DUKE OF YORK'S.

As we note under other illustrations of "The Yellow Jacket," the Property-Man is the most important person concerned in "The Yellow Jacket," and know it! He provides everything, from the ladder which is the path to heaven to a mighty mountain of tables and stools, from a red bag to represent a severed head to a willow tree which is no more than a bamboo, from snow to spider's-web, from silken chariot to silken battlements. He is on the stage throughout, and is supposed to be "intensely invisible" to the audience.

CARICATURED BY H. M. BATEMAN.

MDLLE. POLAIRE AND M. GEORGES BAUD IN 'LE VISITEUR'.

Spence and myself to make sure of doing their play. They evidently realized what good publicity it meant for them.

This was a most interesting period for me. For eighteen months I hardly ever missed a 'first night' and sometimes had two in a week, and as the theatre at that time was in process of changing I was able to see some memorable productions. To do my drawings I had to make rapid notes in the semi-darkness of the stalls and work them out afterwards, and if the opening night of a piece came close to publishing day at *The Sketch* it was sometimes a rush to get them finished in time. There were times when I attended a 'first night' and the sketches had to be in the office by the following midday.

My treatment of these subjects varied somewhat according to the nature of the play we were reviewing, but whether it was a tragedy or a farce I caricatured the principal characters as spiritedly as possible, and I think the more important an actor or actress happened to be the more I tried to get into my drawing of them. There would be perhaps a production by Beerbohm Tree, and the following week one by George Alexander, with Mrs Patrick Campbell or Irene Vanbrugh as leading lady. Next might come a Gerald du Maurier or Charles Hawtrey comedy. These I would treat by drawing the two or three principals large on the page. A Granville-Barker production usually had a good deal of incident in it, which called for a number of smaller drawings and if, as sometimes, we did a music hall or revue . . . my page would be smothered with many little sketches depicting as many of the incidents as possible.

Monocle's reviews could be extremely funny, and were always pertinent. He adopted a light-hearted bantering tone very much in keeping with the spirit of Edwardian burlesque writing. He called Bateman 'our young artist,' and enjoyed putting gently teasing references to him in the reviews, which Bateman repaid with the occasional caricature. Anything slightly *risqué* always brought forth a little comment from Monocle on the propriety of the 'young artist's' presence – he found his young colleague modest and slightly straight-laced – but it was all done in the most gentle way. They went together to see a farce, adapted from the French, called *Oh I Say!* and Monocle wrote, 'It may be rather rather in places; indeed I noticed that many a blush mantled the cheeks of our pale young artist, who sat beside me.'[2]

The old critic and the young artist became good friends. They went out playing golf together – Bateman proving far the stronger of the two – and Monocle enjoyed the younger man's enthusiasm for his sport, for the theatre, and his work. He wrote that Bateman was 'bright and buoyant': he entered body and soul into his cartoons, and gave himself entirely to the things that interested him. Monocle recognized the true enthusiast in him, and at the same time realized he was a little apart. He immersed himself entirely in his interests, but was a watcher of other men. Though he enjoyed sport, his games were never team games. Though he got much out of his clubs, he was never the club type. At the end of a review they did of the Chelsea Arts Ball, in March 1913, Monocle noted in his usual half-teasing way, 'But I looked in vain in the Press box for our artist. Where was he? Perhaps he surveyed mankind concealed as a penguin; or was he taking notes from inside the bull? And there was a very suspicious looking ambulatory lamp-post. I wonder.'[3]

In his work for *The Sketch* Bateman was to some extent using the form inherited from his predecessor at *The Bystander*, Norman Morrow. Again, though his style was his own, he stood in the tradition of theatrical caricaturists – notably S. H. Sime and Henry Ospovat – and was influenced by them, and by Ospovat especially. The change he wrought on *The Sketch*, however, was considerable. Before his arrival, the theatre page and Monocle's reviews were illustrated with photographs, which were terribly dull, static and humourless. As soon as Bateman started with his sketches and caricatures the whole paper seemed to brighten and become more lively. The tremendous vitality of his work immediately arrested the attention. Small wonder that he was in great demand among managers as an advertiser of their plays – and they did not even have to pay him.

He was sometimes asked to take a more direct part in promoting a production, by designing posters or playbills. Most interesting among these were two posters, both drawn in 1912, for plays by Bernard Shaw: *John Bull's Other Island* and *Fanny's First Play*. After *Fanny's First Play* had been running for a little time, at the Adelphi Theatre in London, the management, being rather disappointed with the receipts, wrote to Bateman asking if he would consider doing a poster for the play, to give it a boost. They left it entirely to him to pick on some aspect of the play which he thought would be suitable, but as he sat through it his spirits began to sink. It seemed to him to be all talk and no action, and he left the theatre with no formed ideas. Later, as he thought about it, he realized the play hinged upon an incident which did not actually occur onstage – a young Frenchman kicking an English policeman '*à la savate*' – and it was this that he drew. The management were delighted with it, and the poster was soon on display all over London. The box office receipts rose impressively, and the play became a success.[4]

Not long after this, Bateman was summoned to the Kingsway Theatre, where *John Bull's Other Island* was just about to start. Bernard Shaw had been so pleased with the *Fanny* poster that he specifically asked the management to make sure they got Bateman to do one again. But this time Shaw, who could never resist airing his own views, had executed a sketch to show Bateman how the thing should be done. It was a dreadful drawing, and Bateman had not even seen the play yet, but the manager was so insistent that Shaw's sketch should be followed that even after he had seen the play Bateman decided he might as well keep everyone happy and do as asked. He worked on the poster without inspiration, and, predictably, it was not as well received as the first had been.

At the beginning of April 1914, Bateman resigned his position with *The Sketch*. The working at night and the continual pressure to produce original and amusing drawings on sometimes rather similar subjects had tired him out, and he needed a change, so he went to France, to sketch and

'SPORTING WITH WINTER-SPORTS: BATEMAN ECCENTRICITIES' (V) 'Lugeing: The Achtung-ers', *The Sketch*, 13 March 1912. At this time tobogganing was known as lugeing. The two figures in the centre of the cartoon are Frank Hart and Bateman's sister, Phyllis.

'MONSIEUR L'AGENT.'
The Paris *gendarme* according to H. M. Bateman. *The Bystander*, 25 January 1911.

to fish. This was not the first time he had been to France. Soon after his trip to Holland he had spent some weeks in Paris, and had returned two or three times since. He filled his sketch-books with Parisian street scenes, French cafés, policemen, waiters, the *bourgeoisie*, and many of the sketches appeared transformed later as cartoons. He had also gone on a wintersports holiday to St Moritz with his sister Phyllis, Frank Hart, and some other friends, and again cartoons soon appeared in *The Sketch* – all toboggans and skis – though this time they were for the most part based on a set of photographs he had taken. Everyone was fascinated by these cartoons, as wintersports were then a new and particularly English discovery. Before Edwardian times, mountains covered in snow were rather a nuisance, and best left to the locals who, from necessity, had to cross them on pieces of wood, which was very curious but well documented: nobody had seriously considered there could be much fun in it.

Now, in 1914, Bateman spent three months touring on his own through Brittany, travelling mostly by train and an assortment of horse-drawn vehicles, for there were hardly any cars in the remoter areas – only a

Above:
'FANNY'S FIRST PLAY.'

Above Left:
'NATURE LOST IN ART.'
Earnest students of the
famous *quartier latin*.

'GARÇON!'

A MONTMARTRE GARÇON
WITH AN "AFFAIRE".

THE SUPERIOR
GARÇON.

CAFÉ

PARISIAN CAFÉ SCENES
from cartoons which appeared
in *The Sketch* during 1913.

few motor onmibuses, where the roads were good enough. He started off at Pont-Aven, the small seaside village where Gauguin had lived, and, though he had only vaguely heard of Gauguin, already visitors were arriving from various countries to pay homage to the memory of the great painter, who had died in 1903. After a few days there he struck off into the interior, staying in small hotels from which he would head towards the nearest trout stream to practise his dry-fly-fishing, sometimes with a chance companion, but most usually by himself.[5] These months of solitude, living in quiet country hotels well away from large towns, stopping and moving on when the fancy took him, were essential to him, and such journeys became a regular feature of his life from now on. In Edwardian times there was something of a cult of the countryside: characters in Wells' novels pretended to be gypsies, and Leonard Bast, in Forster's *Howards End*, walked desperately into the country to see a sunrise. But Bateman now began to be really unhappy when in London for long periods, and rushed off into the country whenever he could, as though health and sanity depended on it, which they may well have done. Whether it was Dartmoor or the wilder parts of Spain, as long as the place was really peaceful and remote he felt better.

Rested and healthier though he was after his months of walking and fishing in Brittany, he arrived back in England in July 1914 to rumblings of war. He had just started to settle down to work again when, on August 4, war was declared. And so began four years of misery and confusion for England, for Europe, and for Bateman.

9

AT WAR:
'A HOPELESS DUD'

When war came, Bateman, though worried about his health, shared in the
general buoyant and aggressive mood of the nation, and decided to join up.
The expectation of war had for some years added urgency to public and
political debate, and the German build-up of arms was often the subject of
speculation in the newspapers and in Parliament. It was no surprise,
therefore, when war finally was declared – indeed it was something of a
relief: it broke the tension. Many Englishmen welcomed it with eagerness
and delight – including the poet Rupert Brooke, who wrote, 'Now, God be
thanked Who has matched us with His hour.'[1] Ramsay MacDonald, the
Labour Party leader, a more earthy type, looked not up but down. 'It will
be the most popular war this country has every engaged in. Look out of
your windows and you will see the people beginning to go mad.'[2]
Something like two-and-a-half million men joined up before voluntary
enlistment came to an end in March 1916.

Bateman's decision to enlist did not at first meet with success.

> ... there were at the time only a few vacancies, and as they had waiting
> lists some thousands strong I failed to be noticed among the giants
> from among whom the few men necessary were chosen.

But eventually he 'contrived to push into the London Regiment and for a
time stood up to the routine well enough.'

With all the dreadful casualties of those first years of war, it is difficult
to imagine men clamouring to get to the Front – but they did. As A. J. P.
Taylor has written, 'Enthusiasm brought in more recruits than the
existing military machinery could handle. There were not enough
barracks, often not enough rifles for them. Recruits spent the winter
months in tents and trained with sticks.'[3]

Bateman was such a recruit, and he had to endure bad conditions
during the cold winter months. He soon fell ill with rheumatic fever after
sleeping in a damp camp bed. 'By January of 1915,' he wrote, 'the army
realized me for a hopeless dud and thoughtfully fired me back again into
civil life.'

Bateman's instinctive response to such a 'thoughtful' rejection was to
remove himself as far as possible from humanity, and he immured himself
as a convalescent in a remote inn on Dartmoor. This did not work very
well: he appeared at once to seek to be alone and yet to want the comfort
and reassurance of others about him. He wrote that it was 'very healthy but

very lonely,' and soon returned to town. There, indeed, people congregated, but only to remind him that he had been set aside from the main business of the time.

Young men not in the Forces needed to explain themselves, and though his excuse was valid, and deserved considerable sympathy, he suffered a dreadful battering from his own complex of feelings. The general tenor of the public reaction to men not serving in those first years of war can be gauged from the frequent magazine articles and sour jokes aimed at them. They had to endure what was almost a public humiliation. Civilians were an inferior breed, and the Government's advertisements for enlistment took the form of a particularly vicious psychological campaign.

GLOOM

A typical cartoon of the time, by Dana Gibson, the American cartoonist, and creator of the 'Gibson Girl,' appeared in *London Opinion* in February 1915: a good-looking young couple sit at a table reading a magazine called *War Pictures*. He says: 'They seem to suffer greatly in the trenches from cold feet.' She replies: 'I am glad you sympathize with your fellow sufferers from cold feet.' It is a silly joke, but such things put men like Bateman immediately on the defensive.

Opposite:
'A FEW SPLENDID FELLOWS.'

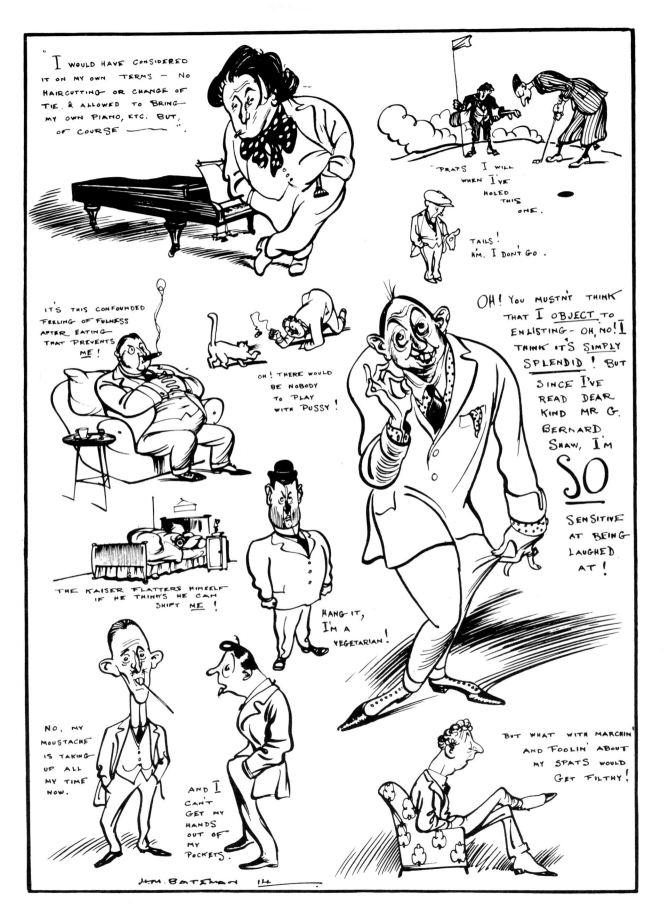

The whole situation was compounded by his own attitude towards those who did not go to war. He had come out publicly at the beginning of the War and condemned those who did not take part. He now found himself one of them, and so condemned himself too. He wrote, 'The years that followed were little better than a nightmare for I suffered much from debility and the depression which goes with it.'

At a later stage in the War, after conscription was introduced, he had to undergo further humiliation, when, 'in company with other doubtfuls, I was made to hop naked and submit to a bombardment of tests before a glaring army doctor sternly ordered me to "Go away and get some clothes on," as if I was responsible for appearing before him in that condition. And in return for my afternoon's exhibition I was handed an unhealthy looking card bearing the magic symbol of C.3. I had done what I could to convert myself into cannon fodder. I just wasn't fit for it.'

The mental dislocation which resulted from these experiences was unfortunately coupled with a literal dislocation. Bateman's family had left Clapham in the early part of the War, and moved to Bromley, in Kent, to escape the bombing. The First War is not perhaps associated with bombing raids on London, but they did take place, and proved both deadly and demoralizing. It was not unusual for Londoners to move out, surprised and angry at this new development in warfare. So Bateman found himself with no settled base in London, and though perhaps, at twenty-eight, it was time for him to leave his parents' home, it was not a good moment for him to have done so. He moved from place to place in London, being, as he said, 'too restless to settle anywhere for long.'

Most of his old friends were away serving, and he spent a lot of his spare time at the Chelsea Arts Club, in the company of the few who had not gone, or those who were on leave. He gave the club as his address during these years when it was an invaluable sanctuary for him. He moved from one place to another, in and around Chelsea, which was still an artists' colony, staying for a while in Frank Hart's studio – Hart had enlisted – where he did 'a lot of work in a rather hysterical condition, being up one day and down the next.'[4]

But his life would have been far more desperate had it not been for the people who did rally round and support him. In his autobiography he mentions the kindness of his friends, the Connards, and of Fred Pegram, one of the original founders of the Chelsea Arts Club, and 'most charming of black-and-white artists, [who] stood by me nobly and lent me a helping hand more than once in keeping up my spirits.'

It was, however, the friendship with William Caine, that developed during the War, which was his mainstay and support. They had met at George Sheringham's house in Hampstead, where Caine also lived, probably during 1912, when the first drawings of Caine appear in Bateman's sketch-books. Caine was some fourteen years older than Bateman, and came from a very different background. His father had been a Liberal MP, and a JP, and had worked in Gladstone's administration as Civil Lord of the Admiralty. He was also President of the British Temperance League. William Caine had gone to Westminster School, where he had worked for the Bar. He then practised for seven years as a barrister, before giving up to start as a writer.

WILLIAM CAINE.

Best known for his short stories, which appeared in many magazines, especially *Pearson's*, he also wrote novels – more than thirty, in fact, between 1909 and 1925. He achieved a significant reputation through his writing, his first book, *Boom*, running to six editions, though, as Bateman said, 'for some reason or another he failed to make the most of his gifts.' His books are clever and witty, and have that whimsical quality that also coloured much of Bateman's work. They had indeed much in common, both in temperament and in outlook. Both were shy, quiet men, united by a love of the country and of fishing: Caine wrote *An Angler at Large* in 1911. They went on frequent fishing and painting trips together, Caine being also a skilful watercolourist. In the Foreword to Caine's book *The Glutton's Mirror* (see p. 64) Stephen Graham wrote, 'He never studied art unless it was through the eyes of his friend H. M. Bateman, with whom he was greatly associated.' The pictures in that book actually show little debt to Bateman, and other of Caine's works that Bateman kept give evidence of a lively and original, if sometimes off-beat, creativity. There is, for instance, a small caricature sculpture after the French fashion, rather grotesque but very animated, showing a small goblin-like creature about to cleave another's head with an axe.

Caine was kindly and perceptive enough to have been of great value to Bateman, who enjoyed his criticism and comments. 'He was a keen critic and never failed to speak his mind about anything I had on the go;' he was a 'kindly genius,' and had 'a splendid character, something so real, so sterling. . . . He was also sympathetic and understanding, a good listener and a good talker, by no means an egoist. Indeed his personal shyness and modesty might even be accounted a failing.'[5] These qualities of sympathy and understanding, kindliness and humour, appear over and over again in Bateman's record of their relationship, which was almost wholly pictorial. Unlike his friend, Bateman was without doubt egotistical, but he quite understood the role Caine played in their relationship, and was deeply grateful to him.

Once again Bateman's preoccupations become the material for his work, and Caine appears as the frequent hero of his cartoons. He wrote:

> I did hundreds of caricatures of him, which I know he loved, and I often introduced him into my published drawings, until people who did not know the inside of the matter began to ask who this queer type I used so often was intended for. Eventually I was able to draw him with my eyes shut.

In the many guises in which he appears, Caine is slightly eccentric, often rather a misfit, but always a delightful character, whom Bateman obviously cherished. Perhaps more than anything else it was ill-health that brought them close: they were 'crocks together,' Caine suffering from a heart condition which his fondness for good food can have done little to alleviate, and their companionship gained strength from this weakness. They thoroughly understood one another.

Friendship and similarity, and the fact that they were both humorous artists, led inevitably to collaboration. Bateman designed some of the jackets for Caine's books, as well as illustrating these and many of Caine's short stories.

BATEMAN BY CAINE.

CAINE BY BATEMAN.

Opposite:
'SOME SOCIAL VIRTUES: SYMPATHY.'
The figure holding the bucket
is William Caine – his role as
sympathetic listener.

Bateman did much illustration in his time (see Bibliography), but it was never really his strongest point. He needed to create his own compositions, and if part or most of the characterization was done for him in the literature, his drawings lost much of their strength. He had to be in at the beginning of the imaginative act – which is why he did not often take up the suggestions for cartoons he received from admirers all over the world. His drawings for Caine's books and stories are nevertheless among the best of his illustrative work.

If Bateman's relationship with Caine was his crutch and support during these difficult years of the War, work itself was his therapy: 'mercifully I could work – it is less exhausting physically to wield a pen than to carry a rifle and equipment – and I threw myself heart and soul into drawing, because it was about the only thing for me to do.'

The variety and volume of his work at this time show an artist deluged with ideas – creative, original, and experimental in his approach. His work was also, of course, a way – his way – of expressing himself not only artistically but temperamentally. It would be wrong to suggest that every cartoon he now produced reads like a book of his own travail, but there are certain apparent themes that reflect his disposition at this time. There is, especially, a certain feeling of uneasiness and guilt, not difficult to understand. He felt he had failed in not becoming a soldier and that his work was somehow an insufficient justification for his existence. In his autobiography he is at pains to show that, while he made money, he was 'no war profiteer.'

> It may be supposed that I was accumulating a fortune during this time, but such was not the case. I never received more than twelve guineas for a page drawing, no matter how elaborate, until well into 1918 and by far the majority averaged about half this amount, and against this there were working and living expenses.

This sense of guilt at being able to earn a living while his friends were away fighting and dying was compounded by a slight brush he had with the Inland Revenue (see chapter 16), and in 1916, perhaps the most creative and most miserable year of his life, there appeared a group of cartoons which focus on the workings of guilt, or the awful effects of retribution.

In December 1916 and January 1917, there appeared in *Punch*, in complete contrast to its other contributions, 'The Man Who filled his Fountain Pen with the Hotel Ink' and 'The False Income Tax Return.' The first is a beautifully melodramatic little story, with a black Mephistophelian figure set against the barest pencil-line background, the second a proper parable, full of moral incident.

The best-known cartoon of 1916, however, must be 'The Boy who breathed on the Glass in the British Museum,' a modern tale of crime and punishment. This appeared in *Punch* on October 4, 1916. It was Bateman's first cartoon for the magazine – an honour and a signal that he had truly 'arrived' as a cartoonist. Although *Punch* was rather slow in taking him up, being always a conservative magazine, more credit to it for introducing him with a cartoon of such power. It comes almost as a shock to discover it among those predictable pages – stark, rather bitter, and far more brilliant than any of those comfortable cartoons that remind one of

Opposite:
'The Man Who Filled His Fountain Pen with the Hotel Ink.'
Punch, 6 December 1916.

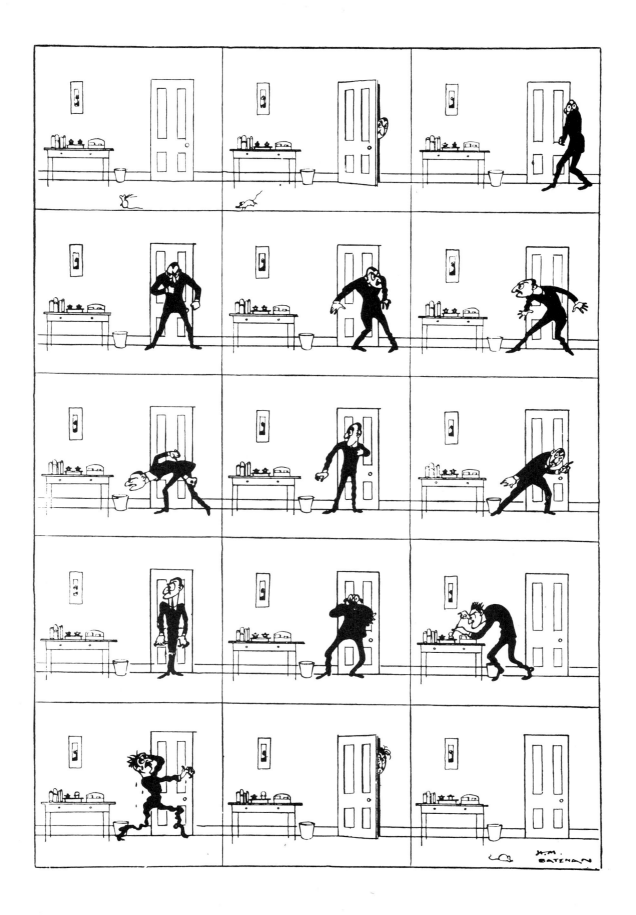

'The False Income Tax Return –

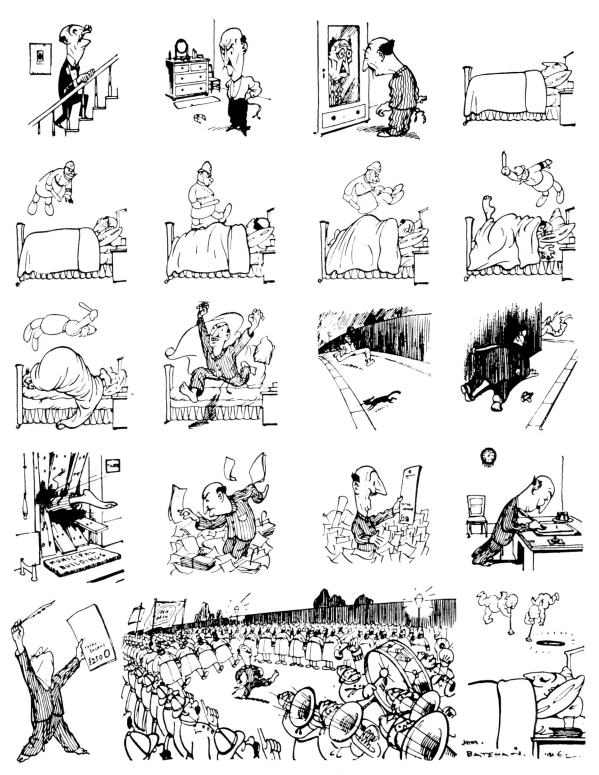

AND ITS RECTIFICATION', *Punch Almanack*, 1917.

rainy Sunday afternoons by the fire. This is not to say that *Punch* did not have good artists in its pages. It had some of the best. During 1916 alone, G. L. Stampa, Frank Reynolds, Frank Hart, F. H. Townsend, George Belcher, Raven-Hill, H. M. Brock, George Morrow, Claude Shepperson, Fred Pegram, G. D. Armour, Bernard Partridge all contributed. Though many were good draughtsmen, and George Belcher drew some really lovely charcoal sketches at the time, nothing of their work compares for vividness and originality with that which Bateman was producing.[6]

Bateman tells the story of the inspiration for 'The Boy who breathed on the Glass . . .' in his autobiography.

> . . . the idea . . . came during an afternoon I spent there [at the British Museum] with a girl. We marvelled at the care with which mummies, thousands of years old, and pieces of broken stone were preserved, whilst not far away men were slaughtering one another. We remarked upon the vigilance of the aged, but by no means decrepit attendants, and how we were even exhorted not to go too close to the exhibits behind their glass cases. 'It would even be a crime,' one of us exclaimed, 'to breathe lightly on the glass.' At once the idea for the drawing flashed into my mind, and almost the next day I had it all worked out in my head and started to put it down on paper.

The girl he went with was the daughter of some neighbours in Bromley. Bateman had met her briefly while visiting his family. After only a few meetings, none intimate, he proposed to her and she refused him, mainly because he always appeared to be worried about his health. It is likely that this encounter was provoked by his confusion and desperation at the time, for there seems to have been little knowledge and less feeling on either side, but it certainly added to his general depression.

As the War continued, Bateman slowly began to realize that he was not after all as useless as he had at first thought. Magazines like *Punch* were eagerly awaited by the men serving abroad, and played an important part in keeping up their morale and letting them know they were not forgotten. Through the war cartoons of artists such as Bruce Bairnsfather they saw their deeds, their difficulties, and their language becoming part of the national folklore. Many wrote stories, poems and articles, or drew for publication, and so there started a correspondence between the serving soldiers and their countrymen at home. This link was, of course, immensely important to them, and Bateman himself received many letters from soldiers with suggestions for cartoon topics. These letters were more valuable to Bateman than their writers could have known, and they encouraged him greatly.

He should perhaps have realized his true position earlier, for while in hospital with rheumatic fever, following his camp-bed experiences, he had entertained his fellow patients, all of them soldiers, with his drawings and caricatures. When, in July 1917, the hospital (the Third London General, Wandsworth) published its *Gazette*, he featured largely in it. His cartoons, 'After You!' and 'Our Persevering Officials,' were both reproduced, along with a photograph of the artist and a short article entitled 'A Famous Patient.'

H. M. BATEMAN.

Opposite:
'THE BOY WHO BREATHED ON THE GLASS IN THE BRITISH MUSEUM',
Punch, 4 October 1916.

H. M. Bateman enlisted in the early days of the War in the Twenty-Third London Regiment. On the first of March 1915 he was admitted to hospital, for some little time he was a patient in ward 3, and it was from the Third London Hospital he received his final discharge. Such is the brief record of the immurement by illness of one of the most remarkable of modern English artists. Arnold Bennett writing in the *New Statesman* under the pseudonym of 'Sardonyx' says 'Mr Bateman is the one really humorous first class draughtsman on *Punch*. ...' Mr Bateman was discharged before this Gazette came into being, but we are happy to say that the walls of our new Recreation Room are enriched with two or three delightfully characteristic caricatures in colour – that of Cpl Mulock as the tyrannical N.C.O. in charge of the Chain Gang being particularly funny. Rich too in his fantastic humour is the drawing of Sgt Derwent Wood with his henchman F. Wilcoxson fixing up a splint for a straffed microbe under the supervision of Capt Harrison.

These drawings are, unfortunately, now untraceable – but, interestingly, Derwent Wood was a friend from the Chelsea Arts Club, and Bateman refers, in his autobiography, to his 'biting witticisms.' There is, too, a nice caricature of Bateman by Wood, dated 1918, and drawn on Chelsea Arts Club paper. Indeed, the Third London General seems to have been something of a resting place for artists: J. H. Dowd, the black-and-white artist, and a regular contributor to *Punch*, did many of the drawings for the *Gazette*.

Eventually, and belatedly, the War Office took Bateman up, and he was sent on official visits, to gather ideas for his drawings, and to give talks and demonstrations – first to the Navy, at Harwich, where his friend Philip Connard was working as a naval artist, and eventually, in the spring of 1918, to the Front. He wrote:

> ... it was arranged for me to visit the Front in France, where I spent a week at a guest chateau from where I and others were motored to various points of interest. In this way I saw a good deal more of the scene of activities than a great many of the poor fellows who were engaged in it.
>
> An amusing incident occurred when we stopped at St Pol, a headquarters for physical training and bayonet exercises. The Commandant, Colonel Ronald Campbell of the Gordons, hearing that I was in the car outside came rushing out in a state of excitement.
>
> 'Bateman,' he cried, 'you are the spirit of the bayonet!'
>
> I was flabbergasted. I, a miserable little crock, who had already been thrown out of the army, to be likened to the spirit of bayonet fighting! But he dragged me from the car and there, sure enough, on the walls inside were enlargements which had been made of my drawings from *Punch* of men in action with the bayonet, which were being used in actual practice.
>
> Campbell insisted on my spending the night at his headquarters, and when I drew on a blackboard before a large gathering during that evening it was 'The Recruit Who took to it Kindly' which was unanimously called for as a subject.

'THE RECRUIT WHO TOOK TO IT KINDLY', *Punch*, 17 January 1917.

'It's the Same Man!'
Punch, 6 June 1917.

'BETWEEN TWO DOSES TONIC.'

'The Kaiser After the War.'

Curiously enough, after my visits to both the Army and the Navy, I did rather less work dealing with the services than previously. Perhaps my imagination had been checked to a certain extent by coming into contact with the reality.

This 'reality' – the reality of war – has always been notoriously difficult for any artist, let alone a humorous one, to deal with satisfactorily. It has been said that the great failure of twentieth-century European visual art was its inability to find any proper way of describing either war. Like everyone else, the creative artist could make little sense of such destruction, so it is no surprise that Bateman's war cartoons came to an end after his visit to the Front. He was too sensitive to continue to draw cartoons, some of which, however appropriate to the general atmosphere at the outbreak of the War, proved rather bluff and hearty upon closer acquaintance with it. Yet, if such cartoons seem now to strike not quite the right note, their value lay in their ability to cheer their readers. Possibly the most successful of his cartoons that dealt directly with the War, and took it as their subject, were those story-telling cartoons in which his fantasy managed to create little epic tales, complete and unchangeable, like 'Between Two Doses Tonic.' The most warlike of his cartoons were those that appeared during the War but were not about soldiers or military matters, which he treated on the whole more lightly.

It was a peculiarity not only of Bateman but of many English cartoonists that satires upon the Enemy, the Kaiser, German soldiers, the German nature, were never as savage or vitriolic as might have been expected. Bateman's Kaiser, for instance, was always an absurd and comic figure with exaggerated moustaches, eventually humiliated and shown for a ridiculous buffoon, but not, like Napoleon, an eater of children. Bateman's precursors were more extreme.

If, however, he felt that the Kaiser was a joke, there were times when he was less inclined to be humorous, and during these years, as a result of the War and his own deep depression, the character of his work changes, becomes more cynical, more violent, more heavily ironical. Cartoons like 'It's the Same Man!' are not really funny at all, but fierce and rather ambiguous. For Bateman, as for Europe, it was a time of change. Those extravagant rhythmical and graceful Edwardian drawings were no longer appropriate, no longer expressed his disposition. There were other influences at work.

LOGICAL
IMPOSSIBILITIES

The two most important influences upon Bateman's work during the war years were the cartoons of the great French artist Caran d'Ache, and those of a group of German artists who published work in the Munich-based magazine *Simplicissimus*.[1] These two sources of inspiration were by no means entirely separate; the work of Steinlen appeared in both; Olaf Gulbransson, a Norwegian who became the chief artist for *Simplicissimus*, was in some of his work influenced by Caran d'Ache, and there were many such cross-currents. Caran d'Ache had died in 1909, and though *Simplicissimus* was still in circulation Bateman only discovered them both properly long after their initial impact had been felt. Caran d'Ache's work had appeared before 1900 in England, in *Pick-Me-Up* and other magazines, and the influence of his line drawings had already borne some fruit in Phil May's cartoons and Aubrey Beardsley's drawings; there is also a possible echo of his work in some early Bateman cartoons. The main effect, however, came through back numbers of magazines which Bateman bought up and collected: *Simplicissimus* itself, *Gil Blas* and *L'Assiette au Beurre*. These magazines were more intelligent and daring than any British equivalent, except *The Yellow Book*, though this was not a weekly magazine like *Simplicissimus*, which had a regular circulation, during 1904, of 65,000. There were articles on lesbians, cocaine, nudism, alcoholism, poems by Baudelaire and stories by Maupassant, and a definite and sometimes savage satirical message. The intention was to shock and shatter the complacent bourgeois mentality, to castigate the failings of their readers.

This is especially true of *Simplicissimus*, in which the castigation is frequently violent as well as witty and the cartoons are serious and often shocking. What Bateman learnt from them, for which there was no English equivalent, was how to give form to violence – a violence which he felt within himself, and which reflected the conditions of the moment. The cruel pencil line of Thomas Heine, one of the artists who contributed regularly to the German magazine, found its way into Bateman's work – and in that brilliant cartoon 'Mexicans at Play' appears unmistakably in the penultimate image: the ultimate one is Bateman's own finishing touch.

Clearly this cartoon is the work of a man who has changed: it comes after Bateman's second brush with the Army, and its rejection of him, at a time when he was at his most desperate. It could not be more different from, say, the suburban types, or even cartoons of 1914, in subject matter

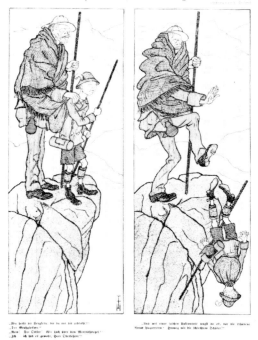

Der Herr Oberlehrer in den Bergen

'DER HERR OBERLEHRER',
a cartoon by Thomas Heine
from *Simplicissimus*.

and style. Yet even now he could produce a cartoon like this and another in an utterly different mode, like 'La Vache a L'espionnage,' almost in the same day. They reflect the seesawing nature of his spirits at the time.

Of all the people who may be said to have affected Bateman's work at one period or another – Phil May, John Hassall, Henry Ospovat *et al* – none had so profound an influence as Caran d'Ache. His real name was Emanuel Poiré, and he was born a Russian, in Moscow, in 1858. His paternal grandfather had been one of Napoleon's officers, wounded at the battle of Moskova during Napoleon's attack on Russia. He had been cared for by some Russians, and had fallen in love with and married a Russian girl. Caran d'Ache was brought up to remember his French ancestry, and as soon as he was old enough he decided to join the French army, eventually becoming attached to the war office. Though he had never had any formal art training, he was helped and advised by Edouard Detaille, and slowly began to publish drawings under the pseudonym of Caran d'Ache, which 'in Russian signifies "lead pencil."'[2]

He loved the army and all things military, and wanted at one time to become a military painter. His first great success, however, came with a highly effective moving silhouette story of the Napoleonic Wars. He produced over four thousand figures and horses, cut out and pasted on to zinc leaf, which when silhouetted by a strong light from behind, and moved around, produced a fascinating drama. The whole action took place across a small white screen, and at each performance was stage-managed

Opposite:
'MEXICANS AT PLAY.'

by the artist alone. He called his silent theatrical '*L'Epopée*,' The Epic, and performed at a small café, *Le Chat Noir*, in Montmartre. It became enormously popular, a great sensation.[3]

Caran d' Ache produced a number of silhouette shows, but also started to publish cartoons in the leading French magazines, and within a short time had established himself as one of the most original cartoonists in Europe, and probably the funniest. The qualities he combined so well and which made him stand out from his contemporaries were those for which Bateman valued him: superb draughtsmanship, and a really original wit. The form he developed to convey his ideas was the strip cartoon without words, and it was the discovery, through Caran d'Ache, of the narrative possibilities of this form that led to Bateman's own great strip cartoons, starting, in 1916, with 'The Boy who breathed on the Glass in the British Museum.'

A Scene From
L'Epopee'
by Caran d'Ache.

Right:
Detail
from a cartoon strip by
Caran d'Ache

Opposite:
'The C.O. A Man's Man.'
Bateman's work clearly
reflects Caran d'Ache's
influence.
Punch, 23 January 1918.

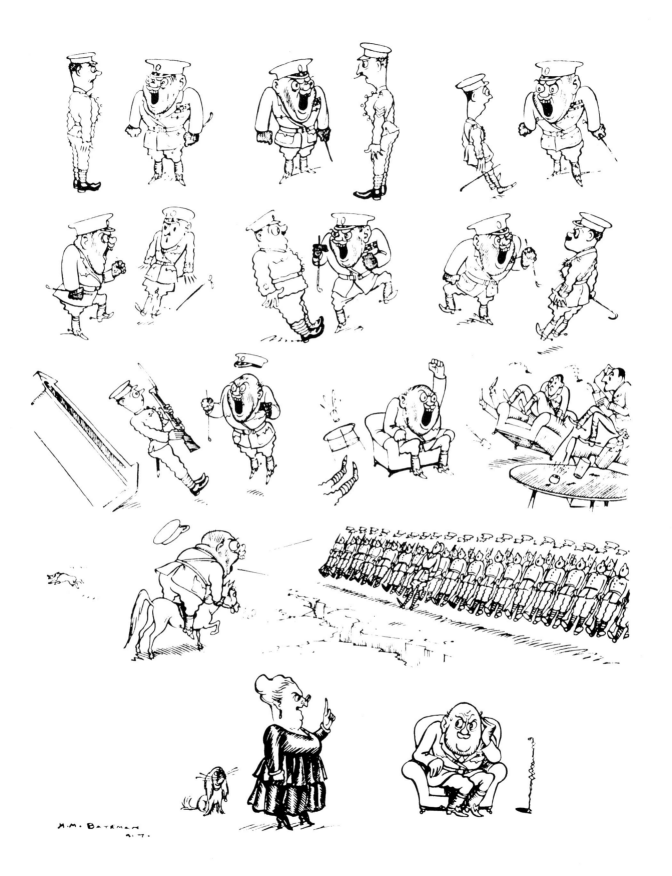

THE EVOLUTION OF A CHRISTMAS CARD

The Art Editor calls on Mr. Bateman

46

'EVOLUTION OF A CARD' – I.

'EVOLUTION OF A CARD' – II.

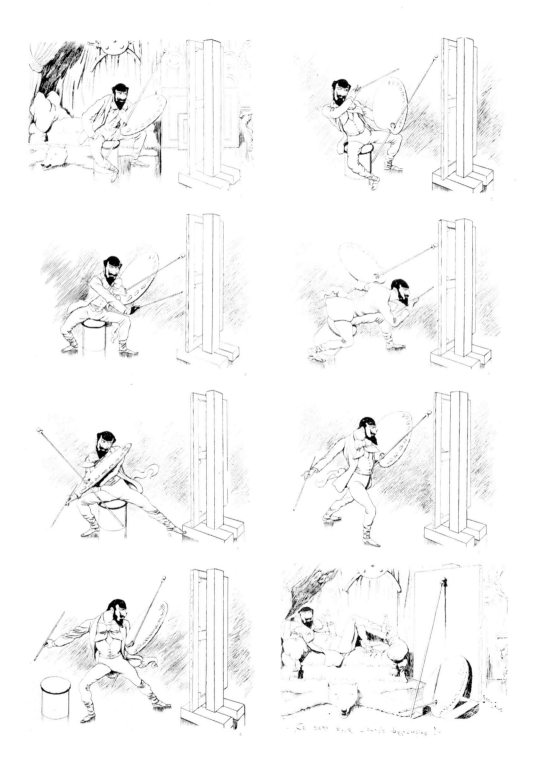

Ce sera pour lundi prochain !

Others had used strip cartoons before – Bateman himself had produced cartoons made up of little incidents like 'The M.P. seeks re-election' or 'A Few Splendid Fellows' – but none had so far used the form as effectively as Caran d'Ache. Partly it was the experience of his proto-cinematic silhouettes that gave him such a grasp on how the essential figure and material in each incident within the story must be selected, then connected to the next, but the choice of the story itself, and the way of telling it, were also peculiarly his own, reflecting a keen eye and a definite liking for the absurd. This struck an answering chord in Bateman, and some of the reason for his wholehearted admiration for the French artist was that there were definite similarities in their areas of interest. The discovery of the strip cartoon, which Bateman really introduced into England in its mature style – without words, that is, not as a comic-strip – was the first and most obvious of his debts to Caran d'Ache, but he owed him many more. Some of his line drawings, for example, between 1916 and 1922 have an unmistakably French atmosphere.

Figures, which had long been mobile, began to shudder in a peculiarly Caran d'Ache way, showing shock, surprise or love through a wavy line. This is a good example of how an idea which Bateman had already anticipated in earlier cartoons was reinforced and consolidated by his contact with Caran d'Ache's work.

Occasionally particular characters were lifted from Caran d'Ache's cartoons to reappear intact in Bateman's own, possibly as a tribute to their originator, but more often he took whole cartoons from Caran d'Ache and transformed them into something very much his own, though still clearly derivative.

There were story-telling devices which Bateman also inherited from Caran d'Ache, and the most noticeable at this time – the one which best fitted his own mood – was the violent denouement.[4] There are a group of cartoons in which Bateman exploits the surprise ending and brings it suddenly upon the reader almost like a physical shock. The cartoons are scripted to lead, through a sequence of seemingly logical events, to an act of great violence, which falls like a blow to the groin.

In 'The Missing Stamp,' or 'The Man Who would not Share the Fire' (in which the figure with the axe is Bateman himself) he has taken a lesson from Caran d'Ache and made it a principle.

The almost surreal logic of the argument or story is also something which, though springing from Bateman's own strange whimsicality, has been influenced by Caran d'Ache. The most famous of Bateman's logical impossibilities is the long cartoon 'The Possibilities of a Vacuum Cleaner,' which appeared in *The Tatler* in 1921, and was later issued as a separate cartoon booklet. Caran d'Ache never produced anything as extensively extreme as this.

Despite the ideas which Bateman took from Caran d'Ache, his drawing style was, in all but a few cartoons, very much his own. His line was more fluid than that of Caran d'Ache, who preferred to have his cartoons reproduced by woodblock, and gave to his characters, though they were full of vitality, a strangely manipulated quality.

The period during which Bateman was most under the influence of Caran d'Ache coincided with his own most original and creative period: a

Opposite:
'LE CHEF D'OEUVRE ATTENDU.' Caran d'Ache's original on which Bateman's 'Evolution of a Card' was based.

'THE MISSING STAMP',
Punch, 11 January 1922.

'Duel Without Fatal Result.'

'Duel With Fatal Result.'
Caran d'Ache's use of
the violent *dénouement*.

'The Possibilities of a Vacuum Cleaner' – I.

'The Possibilities of a Vacuum Cleaner' – II.

'The Possibilities of a Vacuum Cleaner' – III.

'THE POSSIBILITIES OF A VACUUM CLEANER' – IV.
The Tatler, 1922.

time when he was experimenting with various ideas and styles, and becoming master of many forms. During the War he produced a number of cartoons which were quite free of the influence of Caran d'Ache, and so those which show an obvious debt are subsumed in a diverse body of work. In many of the most successful, however, he was mindful still of the lessons he had learnt. Bateman wrote an Introduction to a selection of Caran d'Ache's work in which he paid tribute to him.

> I think it is useless to try to discover who invented the first strip pictures – they were probably done quite a thousand or more years ago – but one thing is certain, Caran d'Ache was the greatest master of the art of telling a story in pictures, without words or with the aid of a very few words, and, so far as I am aware, he produced until quite recent times infinitely more of this class of work than any other artist working in the same vein. He combined perfection in telling a really droll story with superb draughtsmanship and an astonishing observation and knowledge of humanity.
>
> It must not be supposed, however, that Caran d'Ache devoted himself entirely to the story without words. His work was, within its scope, very varied, and he made hundreds of drawings of personalities, illustrations for text and single subjects . . . in all of which he brought to bear a complete mastery of his subject. For me he defies criticism – I simply admire.[5]

II
YEARS OF
ACHIEVEMENT

EXHIBITIONS AND BOOKS

For Bateman, the 1920s were years of achievement, success, and reputation. It was during this period that he became a household name, many of his creations passing into the mythology of the nation. There were exhibitions of his work, articles and reviews, and books of cartoons, as well as the regular appearances in *Punch*, *The Tatler*, and other magazines.

In 1919 an exhibition of his work opened at the Leicester Galleries in London, to scenes rather like those which greet the opening of some long-awaited interstellar drama at the cinema today. Queues formed outside the gallery and down the street, and for the whole period of the exhibition the place was full of people jostling and bustling and laughing. To Bateman, usually so removed from his public, reclusive, yet with an urge for applause that had, at an earlier time, almost led him on to the stage, it was a revelation. After the War, a time of great unhappiness, of debility, of loneliness, this enthusiastic public reaction to his work acted like a tonic, and helped to moderate his 'rather pessimistic outlook.' When he first went into the gallery and saw what was happening it overwhelmed him, and he wept. Thereafter he would sneak in whenever he could spare a moment, and stand unobtrusively in a corner, not announcing himself, watching the crowds and listening to the 'satisfying music' of their laughter. It was all such a success that the gallery gave him another show in 1921. Both exhibitions received enthusiastic reviews in the Press, not only nationally but on the Continent and in America as well.

These reviews led to articles about him and interviews with him, none of them terribly revealing, but almost all emphasizing the unexpected modesty and reserve of the man, in complete contrast to the exuberance and projection of his creations. He now showed himself master of such a variety of styles, controlling such a depth of expression, that few could agree in their efforts to define exactly what he was. Some said that he was obviously a cartoonist, others that he was really a caricaturist; some that his humour was entirely fantastical, others that it was concerned only to reveal reality. The reviewer in *The Bookman* decided that 'he illustrates the human spirit in grotesque allegorical shapes that represent man's thoughts, feelings, passions, the essential individuality that is hidden from us by the orthodox face and figure of the visible person.'[1]

So, with all the laughter, came serious public appraisal. Though the element of social commentary in his work had long been apparent, it was now that the sociological implications behind the comedy seemed important to the public: reflections not so much of the satirical bent of the artist but of the absurdity of society itself.

Bateman's first book of cartoons, published in 1916, and called simply and aptly *Burlesques*, a retrospective of his work since 1912, carried an Introduction by his agent, A. E. Johnson, to whom Bateman was indebted for much sensible advice and help, and who had many of the leading cartoonists on his books – Heath Robinson and Fougasse among them. He was, in fact, deeply involved in the world of illustration and cartoon, and an authority on it, writing a series of books on contemporary artists, called *Brush, Pen and Pencil*, which became something of a standard work. In his Introduction to *Burlesques* the qualities which Johnson emphasized were those of draughtsmanship and comic originality. 'The intensity of the artist's imaginative effort,' he wrote, 'visualizes for us that which humanly cannot be, but would be if it could.' More emphatic was P. V. Bradshaw's essay on Bateman, in his series of pamphlets on *The Art of the Illustrator*, which was also published in 1916, just after *Burlesques*. Bradshaw dwelt upon the cynical side of Bateman's cartoons and, like Johnson, upon his qualities as a draughtsman.[2]

When Bateman's second book of cartoons, *A Book of Drawings*, appeared in 1921 – again a retrospective collection of his work, much of it from the war years – it carried an Introduction by G. K. Chesterton, who took a different line and, in contrast to Johnson and Bradshaw, emphasized the social significance of the cartoons. Chesterton gave intellectual weight to such an approach, and started everyone else off on the same tack – indeed, almost everyone who has written a line on Bateman since 1921, including Bateman himself, has borrowed from this Introduction. Chesterton wrote:

> It is well that a draughtsman with the wild exactitude of Mr Bateman should enjoy one riot of ridiculing modern society; before modern society becomes too ridiculous to be ridiculed. For that is the chief danger at present to this branch of art. . . .

> I am enchanted with Mr Batemen's picture of the War-time Match, and the flaming martyrdom endured by the heroic citizen, in order to observe a special sort of economy. But at least that was in itself a reasonable sort of economy, even if it led in this case to a devotion rather mystical than strictly rational. . . . But . . . suppose Mr Bateman were called upon to draw . . . a policeman putting a very large finger on the lips of a very little boy lest he should whistle, and disturb the repose of the street; while the street, I need hardly say, would be full of motor-buses, brass-bands, backfiring cars, sirens, fog-horns, anti-aircraft artillery, guns going off generally and so on. Well, that wild picture would be a literally and rigidly realistic picture of a real regulation. Living in London, and presumably knowing what the noise of London was like all through the War as much as at any other time, the officials actually did make a regulation that no one should whistle for a taxi-cab; like men anxious lest the grasshopper should indeed become a burden, and his chirp disturb us amid the roaring of lions and the trumpeting of elephants. . . .

Opposite:
'THE WAR-TIME MATCH.'
'ECONOMY IN MATCHES' – I.

This sense that society itself is in the rapids, is already of itself tending to extremes and even extravagancies, has brought a fresher, and in one sense a freer element into our ancient English humour, an element of which Mr Bateman is very typical. It is a telescopic satire, at once logical and ludicrous, which shoots out to the end of any process, and even in exaggerating it, defines it.

'THE GUARDSMAN WHO DROPPED IT.' Probably the most popular cartoon Bateman produced.

Bateman was not only 'typical' he was the leading spirit of this transformation.

A Book of Drawings ran to eight editions, and was quickly followed, in 1922, by *Suburbia*, and *More Drawings*. Altogether ten collections of his cartoons were published between 1916 and 1934: *Burlesques* (1916), *A Book of Drawings* (1921), *Suburbia* (1922), *More Drawings* (1922), *Adventures at Golf* (1923), *A Mixture* (1924), *Colonels* (1925), *Rebound* (1927), *Brought Forward* (1931), and *Considered Trifles* (1934). *More Drawings* contained a selection of work from over the years: Edwardian figures, post-war strip cartoons, a rich variety; while *Suburbia* was something of a return to his old preoccupation with suburban types and customs, with drawings from some of his Edwardian series, alongside vivid line-drawings done especially for the book, in a manner sometimes suggestive of the influence of Caran d'Ache.

Behind all this activity were the weekly cartoons, and in the early part

Opposite: 'ECONOMY IN MATCHES' – II. 16 October 1918.

of 1922 there appeared in *The Tatler* what was probably the single most popular cartoon that Bateman produced, though by no means the best in other terms. It was called 'The Guardsman Who dropped It,' and completely captured the imagination of the public. It also earned for Bateman what was in those days a small fortune: 200 guineas – unprecedented among cartoons. Not unnaturally in these circumstances he quickly followed up in similar vein, and so was born that series of 'Man Who . . .' cartoons which gradually, through the 1920s and early 1930s took over from his other work (see chapter 13) and had such a crucial effect upon his career.

I'll Build a House

Bateman's way of life changed too during 1921, largely as a result of the increased prosperity and self-confidence his post-war status brought him. Shortly after the War, his mother and father finally separated. Their relationship had become more and more difficult, and Bateman, called upon to intervene as his mother's protector and saviour, eventually took a house for her, his sister, and himself in Reigate, Surrey, leaving his father to live the rest of his long life in a small private hotel in Croydon. It is impossible to know exactly what passed, but certainly the impression remains of a mother who, far from needing protection, bent her son's will to her own and carried them all off in an unyielding fit of pique, probably realizing full well that his income could now support such a manoeuvre.

By 1922 Bateman had decided they should remain in Reigate, and engaged an architect to draw up plans for a house, with a purpose-built studio for himself and accommodation for the three of them, on the edge of Reigate Heath. It was a congenial area, surrounded then by lovely countryside, quiet, with a golf course nearby, and not too far from London. And some of his old friends from the Sketch Club had already settled in the area: Edmund Dulac in Reigate, and Heath Robinson in Cranleigh.

The housebuilding drew Bateman into a web of workmen, architects, planners and regulations, and he called the house The Web in ironic commemoration of his experiences. The whole episode, like the cartoons which derive from it, is reminiscent of H. G. Wells' novel *Kipps* when, unable to find anything without narrow winding stairs and smoky little kitchens, Kipps decides to have a house built, and ends up with an eleven-bedroomed villa in seaside Queen Anne-cum-Tudor, every inch of which departed from his original intentions. Bateman's experience was not quite so extreme, but he was obviously made aware of the inherent dangers.

One imagines him strolling over to watch his house being built, keeping a careful and proprietal eye on the workmen, but armed with sketch-book and pencil to record them unobserved. He always loved drawing people at work – some of the most memorable of his early drawings came from the 'Children of Toil' series – but the apotheosis of all Bateman's workmen was conceived at this time, perhaps out of some terrible complication with his drainage system: the plumber.

"I tell you what !" said Bumblefoot in a moment of inspiration, "I'll BUILD a house—that's what I'll do !"

And having come to this decision he got very excited and began to walk about and plan the whole thing in his mind.

And he devoted all his evenings and spare time to the subject and got books on it and a mass of information of every sort dealing with every possible detail, and at last he got the whole thing settled to his satisfaction.

Then he gave himself up to the ecstasy of dreaming about the house that would be his and he revelled in the thought that at last in every way he would have what he liked.

So he called upon the owner of the particular plot he coveted. "I am thinking of building a house," said Bumblefoot, "and want to buy your land." "Delighted," said the owner, "not to say honoured, I'm sure !"

"Yes," continued B., "on the North of the site and facing South." "Oh, I don't like that," replied the Owner quickly, "it must be on the South facing North, or nowhere." And after some discussion, B. agreed, because he liked that site.

Then to the architect of his choice.—"I am thinking of building a hou—" "And you want me to design it for you," chimed the architect immediately. "Why, my dear fellow with all the pleasure in the world." "Splendid," said B., "quite modern, but the general character is to be Tudor." "Oh, I don't like Tudor," snapped the architect. "No, no, not Tudor, anything you like but that—Oh, I can't bear Tudor."

"Now what I propose to give you is something of the Neo Rococco period with a touch of Ante Georgian to relieve the whole; it will be bright without being obtrusive, and the general effect very distinguished. Of course, you can choose all your own fixtures and fittings, but not that horrid old Tudor !" and B. decided to leave it at that.

And so he came to the window maker. "I am building me a house and I particularly want the windows from you." "Certainly," said the window maker, "and in what style." "Metal casements," said B. "Oh, not metal, I don't like metal," said the maker. "Wood or nothing is what you want, Sir !" and again B. gave in

Then the Plumber. "I am making a home of my own and I want you to fix me a bath," said B. "Thank you, Sir," said the Plumber. "What kind of a barf will you 'ave ?" "Porcelain Enamel," said B. "Oh, I don't like Porcelain Enamel," said the Plumber, "fireclay fer me !" and got his own way.

And then he came to the Carpenter. "The woodwork of my house must be of the best." "Of course," said the carpenter. "Oak," said Bumblefoot. "Oh, not Oak ! I can't bear Oak !" said the carpenter. "What you want is Teak," and after considerable discussion B. consented, feeling that the man must know his business.

"I'LL BUILD A HOUSE"—I

Then he went to the Builder. "I am thinking of building a house and I want you to do the work." "Done," said the Builder, "in what material?" "In red brick," said B. "Oh, no, not in brick! I don't like bricks," replied the Builder. "Stone is the only material I consider fit for houses." And B. felt bound to agree when he heard the arguments in its favour.

And at last the Gardener. "I want you to lay out a garden for me," said B. "A sweet, peaceful and typically English garden, with roses and—" "Not roses," put in the Gardener immediately. "I don't like roses or suchlike, I specialise in Rockery." And he very quickly convinced B. and won him over.

And there came a day when all the details had been settled and all the parties concerned were gathered together on the site. "Well, Gentlemen," said B. "I am glad to say that we have all come to an amicable agreement in this matter. There is only one request I have now to make of you, and it is that you will erect the building and complete the work in the shortest possible space of time." "No! No!" shrieked the constructors in chorus, "We don't like working quickly—it's wrong, wicked, it can't be allowed!" And Bumblefoot, who by now was quite broken in, speedily gave way before the facts as they were presented to him.

"...k Heaven," he murmured as in course of time he came to be wheeled into the completed domain——

"They all got what they LIKED!"

"I'LL BUILD A HOUSE."—II

'Something Wrong. The Plumber Fixes It' – 1.

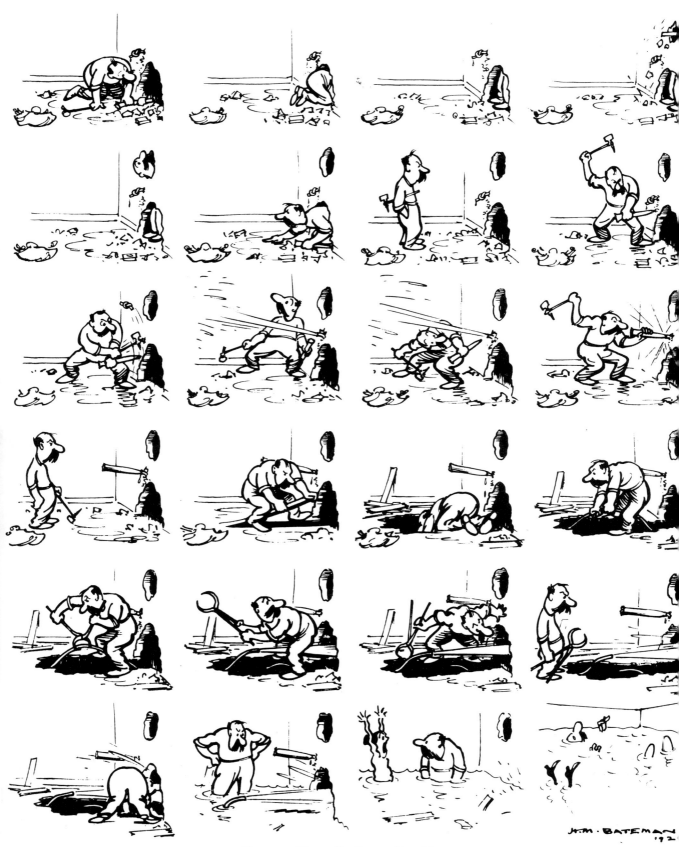

'SOMETHING WRONG. THE PLUMBER FIXES IT' – II.
Punch, 31 January 1923.

RADIOS AND MOTOR CARS

Bateman's new lifestyle as a man of means and property inevitably led to a slight shift in the focus of his attention: he began to acquire the possessions and also the preoccupations common to the householder, and, as always, this became material for his work. The Twenties were years of domestic transformation: the new technology of the kitchen was altering the pattern of domestic life. Electricity was becoming more common in the home, people acquired vacuum cleaners (see 'The Possibilities of a Vacuum Cleaner': pages 112–15) and stoves that no longer required a lifetime of servitude and a bevy of little girls to keep clean and alight.

However, perhaps the most significant of all new possessions in the Twenties, which was soon considered essential, was the radio – or the wireless, as it was then known. Bateman was fascinated by the wireless, and gave all his enthusiasm to it. He drew covers for the *Radio Times* in its early days, and wrote humorous articles for *The Amplion*, a radio buff's magazine, on the mental aberrations and disturbances in behaviour brought about by the new invention. But above all, of course, he drew cartoons.

It is difficult now to appreciate the complete transformation that radio brought about. It was a sudden sense of community, of liveliness, of laughter, entertainment and culture, all within one's own four walls. And in a remarkably short space of time, despite certain imperfections in reception, and what was, by today's standards, incredibly bulky equipment, there was hardly a family in the land without a 'wireless set.' It was the symbol of the period between the wars: 'In everybody's backyard stood an enormous pole with a thickish wire like a clothes line leading to a chimney or under the eaves, and the suburbs became a tangle of aerials.'[2] Talk was all of rheostats, valves, variometers and oscillators, and evenings were consumed with endless searching of the wavelengths, trying to get Prague, Warsaw, the Hague, or Berlin. These were the great years of broadcasting, before 1928 and the coming of sound in film.

The image given to history by the Twenties, the 'roaring Twenties,' was imposed on it by a tiny fraction of the populace which managed to attract inordinate coverage in the Press. But the backdrop against which all the high jinks were played out really did exist in some depth, and nothing perhaps evokes the Twenties so much as its music – especially its dance music. The introduction of the radio (the first regular broadcasting began with London 2LO in 1922) helped to strengthen enormously the hold contemporary music had over the population – Noel Coward spoke of the 'potency of cheap music' – and it was not just the young, as it is to a great extent now, who were affected. It was said, for instance, that no restaurant could hope to survive without a dance floor: Lyons Corner House had four – indeed the band of the Savoy Hotel, the Savoy Orpheans, was one of the most popular dance bands in the country, and the first to broadcast. Dancing, popularized by the radio, and available everywhere, became for some almost a way of life, with *thé dansant* and night clubs sprouting all over the cities.

'The Dancing Girls' Paradise',
Punch Almanack, November 1924.

Opposite:
'The Hotel Radio',
Punch, 29 April 1936.

Though Bateman recorded such aspects of his contemporary environment, now, living out of London, and becoming increasingly rather staid and serious, most of the dancing and the music seems to have passed him by. Certainly he still kept up his tap-dancing, but in the privacy of his own home. His dancers and musicians are drawn with rhythm and grace, but they were not now an integral part of his existence, a key to his vision of the world, as was the case before the War. Even on his visit to the United States in 1923, the centre of modern music (the Charleston was not danced in London until 1925) he seems to have avoided such excitements, preferring to go off into the countryside, sketching the natives. (See chapter 14.) He participated more fully in other, less extrovert pastimes.

One of his chief pleasures during the Twenties was motoring. On moving to Reigate, he bought a Riley Minerva – one of 250 different makes of car then on the market, in the days before the giant manufacturers swallowed up the smaller firms. The function of the motor car then was almost entirely to give pleasure, and Bateman, like everyone else who could afford it, would go on motoring tours around the country, driving through what was still a pre-motor car landscape. (The first petrol station opened in 1920, the first traffic lights appeared in 1927.) He would motor over to Cranleigh, to see Heath Robinson, or travel down to Devon, to see James Thorpe, and tour round Cornwall with him. In his *English History 1914–1945*, A. J. P. Taylor wrote that 'The motor car was undoubtedly the great formative influence of the new England, transforming social life even more fundamentally than the railways had done before it. In 1920 the number of private cars registered was 200,000. Ten years later it exceeded a million, and reached nearly two million by the outbreak of the Second World War.' The motor car had unprecedented effects on mobility, status and courtship – Bateman himself proposed marriage in the back of his Minerva – and as well as altering for ever the face of the country, had certain alarming effects upon the behaviour of its inhabitants, which Bateman noted with some relish.

GOLF AND THE COLONELS

In 1923, Methuen, who published all but the last of Bateman's books of cartoons, brought out a collection of his drawings called *Adventures at Golf*, along with a companion volume by Heath Robinson called *Humours at Golf*. Golf was an immensely topical subject – all the contemporary magazines were full of it: serious discussions, funny stories, cartoons and photographs of golfers, or of people who, even if they did not play the game, dressed as though they did. It was a national enthusiasm far more popular then, in its first flush, than it is today. Bateman himself was a keen golfer, and chose the site for his house partly because of its proximity to the local course.

The golfing craze had quickly swept the country. By 1911 *Punch*, in its review of the previous decade, could report that 'not to play put one completely outside the pale' – though only thirty years before, it had been 'an almost wholly Scottish game.'[3] Golf clubs and golf courses now proliferated. By the Twenties golf had worked its way into literature: H. G. Wells, in his novel *Bealby* describes an encounter with a drunken golfer suffering the effects of the nineteenth hole, and Galsworthy numbered the game, along with sitting in draughts and revising the prayer book, as 'a passion of the English.'

Bateman began to play golf at about the time he began to draw for publication, in 1903. Even before this, while still at school, attracted by the obsessive nature of the game, he had drawn comic pictures of golfers weighed down by enormous bags of clubs, trudging through the pouring rain, grimly determined. The span of his golfing cartoons is the span of his working life as a cartoonist, and therefore they offer, if not always as powerfully as the best of his more individual creations, a simplified and continuous commentary of his development as a cartoonist.

'The Man You Give a Game To',
Punch, 16 October 1920.

'I'LL GET A CAR',
The Tatler, October 1923.

Many of his Edwardian golfing cartoons show the great golfing heroes of the day: James Taylor, J. H. Braid and Harry Vardon – The Great Triumvirate, as they were known – and especially Braid, whose long loose form and bristling moustache appear a number of times. But perhaps no single person, apart from the Prince of Wales, popularized the game more than A. J. Balfour, the Unionist Prime Minister between 1902 and 1905 – brilliant, charming and aristocratic, though not a success as a head of Government, and called by Clemenceau *'cette vieille fille.'* Bateman saw him play and sketched him with various select and admiring members of the public in the background. He was also commemorated in a book of golfing poems by Robert K. Risk – a regular contributor of humorous songs and poems to *Punch* and other magazines – for which Bateman provided the illustrations.

As I was loafin' along the links, an' smokin' my pipe the while,
    I seed a man who was goin' round with a most umbrageous smile,
'E was knockin' the sand off 'is niblick-'ead, and I sez to 'im,
    'Oo are you?'
Sez 'e 'I'm a Golfer, – a very fair Golfer – Golfer and Statesman, too.'
    Now 'is work begins at Gawd knows when, an' 'is work is never through;
'E ain't no reglar sportin' toff, nor 'e ain't no professional too,
    'Es a kind o' a giddy harumfrodite – Golfer an' Statesman, too.[4]

'THE MAN WHO MISSED THE BALL
ON THE FIRST TEE AT
ST ANDREWS',
The Tatler, 1925.

But Bateman was not so much interested in personalities as in the eccentricities, peculiar fanaticisms, and passions which the game brought forth. It became in his cartoons a battleground where man fought against a perverse and unconquerable force, which made fools of the wisest, upset the proud, confounded the vain, and allowed the small and unprepossessing – among whom he counted himself – to humble the mighty. It was a great leveller and slayer of pretentiousness, which conformed with his own purposes as a cartoonist.

Many of his cartoons describe the cultural accretions of golf – the paraphernalia, the club house, the customs – and note that unaccountable dedication to all sorts of ludicrous articles of clothing which marked out the golfer from other mortals.

Though a passionate golfer himself, in his cartoons he made use of the paradox the game offered: to the observer it seemed a most lamentable display of childish inanity, yet to the devotee it acquired a compelling inner logic that made all the usual rules of conduct redundant. The description he gives in his autobiography of his golfing days is entirely taken up with memories of more or less lunatic behaviour.

I did a lot of drawings about golf at which I was rather hot tempered, although positively benign in comparison with some players I encountered. I remember one who was a good player who kept calm so long as things were going well with his game but blew up

completely when reverses came along. On one occasion at a certain hole he played his second shot into a bunker, and on coming up to it found it deeply embedded half-way up the face of the hazard. To get at it he had to plant one leg up above the ball and balance himself precariously on the other, with very little hope of dislodging the ball then. He played the shot saying 'Three!' as he did so, and failed to move the ball an inch. He had another smack at it, crying 'Four!' which again had no effect, and followed this up with a terrible swipe, shouting, 'Five!' when he lost his balance, fell back into the bunker, and lay there on the sand beating the air with his club and continuing to count rapidly 'Six, seven, eight, nine, ten,' and so on.

Another time I was staying in Dorset and went out for a game on the local links. There was only one other man at the clubhouse when I arrived there and we fixed up a game forthwith. He turned out to be an elderly colonel who had just returned to England after a long sojourn in India. He was quite pleasant and normal until a few holes had been played and then I began to feel the atmosphere was becoming somewhat oppressive. I was a better player than he and was giving him several strokes, but in spite of this I had won every hole so far, and as additional handicap for the colonel he had the village idiot for his caddy. This poor creature trailed behind us, sometimes crying, and mumbling something about a burial which had recently taken place, which was distinctly annoying for the colonel who began to play worse and worse. After a particularly bad shot on his part I remarked, perhaps tactlessly, 'I expect you are a bit off your game this morning.' 'Do you wonder,' hissed the colonel, whipping round and waving his arms about the head of the wretched loony, 'it's – it's this *thing*!' Somehow or other, though, he managed to stiffen the youth and for the next few holes there was an almost cheerful air about the game, but there was another incident before the round finished.

The last hole was a blind one and the caddy was sent forward some distance to mark the drives.

'Now, mind,' said the colonel beforehand, 'you watch me on the tee, and just as I drive I will shout "Fore!" and then you are to follow the ball in the air and mark where it stops. Don't you dare to let your attention wander.'

There stood the caddy down the course, mouth open and a vacant look in his eyes, but with his head turned rigidly towards the tee as ordered.

'Fore!' shouted the colonel, and drove. There was a smack, and instantly the caddy's head turned in the direction of the hole, remaining in that position until further orders. But I'm afraid he hadn't marked the ball after all. The colonel had topped it and it had come to rest only a few yards ahead of the tee!

'THE NEW WORD IN GOLF.'

This account sets the tone for many of the golfing cartoons, a number of which portray just such a colonel in different stages of distress, frustration and anger. Perhaps the most notable imprecation in Western art was conceived out of the lips of one of this furious breed.

Bateman's colonels were so successful that in 1925 he published a collection entitled, appropriately enough, *Colonels*, with an Introduction by Harry Graham, who wrote that 'Mr Bateman's Colonel is indeed the only possible, the only perfect Colonel, the paragon, the Colonel of our dreams, the Colonel of our heart's desire. ... Of an abnormally choleric disposition, his talent for vituperation has long made him the envy of his peers. Years of soldiering in the far-flung outposts of Empire (on an exclusive diet of chutney and Bombay duck) have so warped his temper that to live in his society is to dwell on the slope of an active volcano, prone to erupt at the slightest provocation.'

'The Colonel Implores His Daughter to be Reasonable.'

The collection is remarkable not only for the extraordinary force of expression which Bateman controlled within his line, but also for the exact understanding, the literary quality, of the captions. There is a reciprocating humour between words and picture, the contrast between the mildly understated caption and the furious overstatement of the cartoon being in itself much of the joke. This was a condition toward which Bateman was always striving in his cartoons: where caption and drawing are conceived as one, and work together. The drawing is not then the literal illustration of an idea, but inherently humorous; nor is the caption merely a superfluous comment upon the drawing. With his colonels he achieved a perfect balance.

'THE COLONEL FILLS HIS
WADERS.'

Although this collection was not produced until the mid-1920s, there had been many earlier cartoons involving colonels, arising, not unnaturally, out of the war years, when public interest was focused to such a degree upon military matters. The book was published in response to a demand created by Bateman's previous work, and the drawings were produced as a collection, all at the same time, not appearing individually first in magazines. On the origins and development of his colonels, Bateman wrote that he had

... made quite a reputation for drawing colonels, although I had no preconceived intention of developing the subject to the extent I have since done. ... I suppose my rendering of him appealed strongly to most people and they asked for more which I produced, and still more, until egged on by the encouragement I received where the colonel was concerned I followed him into civil life and produced a big set in the form of a book dealing with him in the privacy of his home.

But during the War years I think my admirals, of which I did a good many, had pride of place. The admiral was much fancied then and at the start was certainly leading. I might have continued to draw admirals indefinitely, but the colonel was not to be denied, and forging steadily ahead he outpaced the admiral. ... Incidentally I have made some good friends among colonels and have sometimes marvelled at their even allowing me to speak to them after some of the things I have imputed to them. But there are some who will not face me and I know of one who actually left his home and went away for the time that I was staying with some friends in the same neighbourhood!

THE ART OF DRAWING

In 1926, in contrast to his earlier publications, Bateman produced a little book, most important to himself and well received, called *The Art of Drawing*. It was not in the least humorous, but a simple and direct instruction manual for beginners, and a statement of his own seriousness and creed as an artist. It was a product of his self-assurance at this time, and emphasized his belief in continual application and constant reference to life. He divided the book into three sections: the first called 'Theory,' the second 'Practice,' and the last 'Selection.'

In the first part, he states that drawing is primarily a question of training the eye, and that:

> There may or may not be different ways of achieving an ultimate end, but I will state with confidence that whatever branch of art you may wish to devote yourself to in the long run, the more thorough your knowledge and practice of the rudiments of academic drawing may be, the surer will be your foundations and the greater will be the reserve of strength you have to draw upon, when the time comes for you to make an effort on your own lines.

He goes on to say that drawing is very much in the nature of an 'argument or problem and you cannot do more than argue or discuss this problem until you feel incapable of arguing any further.' The second part of the book consists of actual drawing excercises, but it is the last part, 'Selection,' which reveals most about his own way of work. Sufficient patience and application will allow anyone to draw correctly, but this is merely a 'simple formula for taking measurements with the eye and putting down the results on paper.' The difficult and unteachable thing is 'expressive drawing.'

> You may say that you can see no relation whatever between the methods I have been expounding and my work, with which you are probably familiar in the Press – there is no trace of the very scrupulous attention to detail I have been laying down as the right and proper way to set about making a drawing. On the contrary, the caricature drawings usually consist of a very few lines indeed.
>
> That is quite correct, and the reason for this is that in order to express the numerous ideas with which I have dealt it has been necessary for me to evolve a synthetic treatment, sufficiently elastic to enable me to convey what I have thought necessary to express. In other words, a simple vehicle, or reduction to terms.
>
> It would have been a physical impossibility to have covered the same amount of ground if I had set about it by academic methods, and,

'THE DAMNED SPOT',
Punch, 1916.
'. . . during the war years I
think my admirals, of which
I did a good many, had pride
of place . . .'

moreover, where the primary intention is to entertain, too thorough and elaborate a rendering of external appearances and details may very easily result in the real purpose becoming obscured or entirely missed.

To pass from the academic to the synthetic and still retain realism is a difficult process, calling for great patience and much experiment, and it can only be arrived at by a process of elimination, and more elimination, until all that is not essential has been discarded.

Yet one must say enough. A nice sense of proportion is very necessary here, for it is just as easy to make the mistake of saying too little as too much, and to whittle away beyond a certain limit will mean a flimsy effect of something without any real substance – the essence you are trying to distil will then become devitalized.

That great artist Phil May worked very much on these lines, always aiming to simplify his drawings to as large an extent as possible. But I am not comparing Phil May's work with my own, for his conception was of an entirely different nature. Phil May did not invent. His drawings were always of individuals, each one quite different from the other, and not composite types, such as I have evolved for the purpose of expressing a flight of the imagination.

This calls for selection. You must discover for yourself what is necessary and what is not, to express your subject as a whole.

Having discussed the importance of selection, elimination and emphasis, three closely related principles – by selecting something upon which to focus one automatically eliminates other things and in so doing emphasizes something else – he decided that the three next most important principles, again closely related, to each other and to the first group, were rhythm, movement and gradation of line.

First as to Rhythm. It may well be asked what is rhythm as it applies to drawing and how is it to be achieved? The dictionary definition of it is given as 'Harmonious correlation of parts,' and this, I think, is a very true one. Harmony implies a condition in which composition, technique, and expression are successfully blended.

Rhythm I believe only emerges when considerations of method and technique have been so thoroughly worked out and mastered as to have reached a pitch in practice which may be called definite. By this I mean that this aspect is no longer a tentative and experimental one. . . . I could show you how I draw rhythmically, but that would be because I should be drawing in my own style, and I could perhaps imitate the style of another artist sufficiently to embody rhythm to a certain extent in what I was doing; but I could not show you how to set about a rhythm for your own.

At the same time I believe a golden rule for achieving it is to always bear your subject in mind as a whole and not simply as a collection of parts to be fitted together and joined up – to work with the end in view from the start. To give an example of this let us imagine that you are about to draw a picture in which two figures are seen, with a room as a background. You commence by drawing the head of one of the figures; but whilst you are doing this the whole of what is still to come should be clearly before you in the mind's eye. The rest of the body and the other figure, as well as an idea of the background, is not already actually on the paper, only because your hand has not yet had time to set them down. It is a near approach to thinking of and doing two things at once, and it cannot be done to the fullest degree until the technique and problem of constructive ways and means have been assimilated. When these considerations are so thoroughly under control that they can be, relatively speaking, forgotten, then all your faculties will be given up to expressing the idea as pictured in your mind's eye, with whatever feeling you may be capable of putting into it – you will be recording your emotions with the pencil on paper. . . .

Another aspect to be considered is Movement which for our purpose may be described as the arrested moment; that spark of Life which shows through every vital work, whether it be a portrait or a still life. Odd as it may seem, I would say that a good memory is part of all that goes to this quality, and to train or adapt it in relation to drawing I have found that a good plan is sometimes to take mental photographs, a practice which, even if it does not appear at first to be of any real assistance, is at any rate interesting and so easy to accomplish as to make a few experiments worthwhile.

The process is extremely simple. It amounts only to turning your eyes in the direction of what you are practising upon and then closing the eyes for a few seconds to allow the vision to clear itself, about four seconds being enough for this. Then open them suddenly for about half a second and close them again, when the image will appear in the mind's eye. But it is of no use to do this quite mechanically and expect a good result. It is necessary to be keyed up to the moment of opening the eyes, and whilst they are seeing for that brief period be conscious that you are making an effort to take in all that flashes upon them; then when they are closed down again it is the essentials rather than the details which will come before you. . . .

Another consideration in drawing is that of the Gradation of Line. My own particular style is so very dependent upon this aspect that I am bound to deal with it as something of extreme weight and importance.

Where a manner of drawing has been evolved which is based chiefly upon economy of means in expression these remarks cannot fail to apply, and where the manner is such that economy or simplicity is not a decided characteristic I think the same observations still hold good to a great extent. . . . To put it as simply as possible, it may be said that where it is light in the drawing the line should be thin and where it is dark the line should be thicker. If the style is such that objects are expressed in a continuous flowing line we will take as an example a head, which would be drawn almost in outline, whilst its details – the nostrils, eyes, ears, etc. – would be put into the main outline, also in outline. Assuming the light to be coming from the most usual direction, which is almost above, it would mean that the line would start upon the forehead as thin, for this is well lit, it would thicken slightly towards the brows, for here there is a depression in the formation of the skull inducing shadow, and it would be thin again in following the upper part of the nose, which is again catching light. Naturally it will be thick under the nose, thinner on the upper lip, and thicker under the lower lip, thinner on the chin and again thicker under the chin, and so on. . . . Do not, however, take these instructions too literally, for there will be occasions in line drawing where they cannot be strictly applied in order to produce the effect aimed at. . . .

The character of your line should be a clear and firm one, but it should never be too definitely settled as to its weight and strength – it should have rather an elastic quality. . . .

I have found that an excellent practice is to carry a sketch-book and to make notes of anything which is sufficiently interesting. . . . For many years I was never without a sketch-book within reach, and I would fill in a few odd minutes by making a sketch . . . the sketch-book is one of the most potent and natural forms of training as well as being a valuable record, for use often at unexpected moments long afterwards.

Although *The Art of Drawing* is extremely modest in tone, it was recognized that Bateman was speaking from the heights of considerable accomplishment. His peers as well as his public looked upon him as the master comic draughtsman of the time, and saw in his work a perfect marriage of comic vision and technical ability. John Bohun Lynch, himself a caricaturist, and author of a book on Max Beerbohm, described Bateman as 'the most deservedly popular comic artist of the day.'[5] Cornelius Veth emphasized that 'even when his figures are absurd his drawing is essentially correct.'[6] And his old friend Frank Reynolds wrote that he was 'a considerable artist in the most serious sense. That he has painted interiors, landscape, still life. That he has studied from the life under very able masters and that he has all this at the back of those light-hearted grotesques for which he is famous. But any discerning person who knows this artist's work can see it popping out in every line.'[7]

Bateman himself was never so delighted as when someone complimented him on his drawing of a hand or a foot, a portrait, or the folds in a dress, and he shows in his sketch-books an ability to draw almost any object, animal or person, with equal facility.

Often, his comic drawings were direct developments of these sketches, the comic fantasy firmly rooted in literal representation. P. V. Bradshaw demonstrated this most effectively by collecting all the preliminary sketches for one of Bateman's cartoons and presenting them in sequence.[8] Bradshaw was so impressed by Bateman's ability that he continued to hold him up as an example of versatility and comic inventiveness, and published sheets of his drawings as lessons for the Press Art School, which he founded, in Forest Hill. (Ralph Steadman is perhaps the best-known student of this establishment, which continued to offer postal tuition courses to hopeful cartoonists for more than thirty years.)

The clear understanding of basic technique which Bateman expressed in *The Art of Drawing* was matched at this time by an equally clear realization of the craft and the function of his chosen career. There was no theory which he set out to practise, just ideas evolved out of years of experience. The most cogent expression of his attitude to his art, not only in its relation to the outside world but in its own inner equations of excellence and effect, is found in a lecture he gave to the Royal Society of Arts.[9] He wrote of humorous art – especially black-and-white humorous art – that:

> It is doubtful if the average person realizes to what an extent this highly specialized art has become a part of his everyday life and how much he may, perhaps unconsciously be influenced by it ... his day starts with the newspapers many of which carry a cartoon in a light vein, and probably a comic drawing and short comic strip. As he goes to work and about his work, he sees many light-hearted appeals to buy something or order his life in some way ... if he goes underground he passes through avenues of pictorial appeals, a large proportion of them inspired by the comic spirit. Apparently not satiated with this he buys a magazine for the express purpose of enjoying some concentrated humour. ...
>
> In my own experience I have come to a few conclusions on the matter of the combination of the joke, or idea, with the drawing. I think this can be summed up under three headings. First, a good idea poorly drawn is usually wasted – useless because the presentation has broken down. Second a not so good idea, in fact a quite mild and ordinary one, if accompanied by a really good drawing is well worth while and can stand up strongly. The treatment has a quality of its

own, something which appeals and gives strength to the fragile idea which serves only as an excuse or reason for the good drawing. This carries out the old adage that it is not so much what is said but the way it is said that counts. Thirdly a very good idea and a very good drawing combined may be a masterpiece. . . .

Of these three conditions the first may be ignored altogether – the second is probably the most useful and usual. . . . In my opinion this is how it should be, for comic drawing should not be too dependent upon its subject matter; there should be something inherent in the drawing itself that is funny. If that something is not present the drawing resolves itself into the literal illustration of an idea and is entirely dependent for its humour on a good joke.

Bateman then went on to discuss the merits of Caran d'Ache and Charles Keene, for him the two greatest black-and-white artists, and described certain changes in the art itself since their day.

. . . is it possible to say on what their greatness was founded? There seems to be a clear answer to this. They were draughtsmen first and humorists second. All the work that has stood the test of time has had for its basis sound craftsmanship. Humour changes, the jokes of Keene are now mostly out of date and many of the shafts of Caran d'Ache's wit no longer sting, but their drawing is still valued. . . .

It is not unlikely that as time goes on Phil May will be preserved more for the beauty of his drawing than for his fun. The humour until about the period of Phil May's death was incidental; he and many of his forerunners had a very plain and straightforward job in their work: they had only to draw the people they met or saw about them; generally speaking there was little invention. But after Phil May a change began to set in, imagination and fantasy began to gain ground. . . . The old conventional method of literal illustration of a joke went on – it exists to this day – but accent on the thing seen became less of an essential and gave way to some extent to the thing imagined. The audience began to join in and meet the performers half way. . . . The audience had become more sensitive to fine points and inflections, so that the problems for the humorist grew easier in some ways and more difficult in others, as the field widened and the public became aware of and approved the increasing developments in the art.

Bateman, who started to draw for publication in the year in which Phil May died, 1903, was in the very forefront of this change. Though he only drew what appealed to and interested him, he did see himself as something of a social historian, and to some extent deliberately set out to make a record of the age.

It is certain that the comic artist records almost daily the manners, customs and spirit of his age, in ways not to be found so vividly, or readily, among the treasures of museums and galleries devoted to serious art.

His continual insistence upon academic drawing skills, however sensible in itself, was part of a deeply conservative attitude towards art. Despite the fact that in his own way he was an innovator, a creative artist of originality,

'BROTHER BRUSHES' – I.

'Brother Brushes' – II.
'A deeply conservative attitude towards Art.'

he, like many of his contemporaries, distrusted the trends in modern art which led away from the figurative towards abstraction. In 1910, at Roger Fry's famous Grafton Street exhibition of post-impressionists, Bateman had drawn cartoons making fun of the paintings, and later, at the 1914 futurist exhibition, had done the same thing. He showed little understanding of or sympathy for these movements, though later in life he came to value some of the post-impressionist painters. It has been said that part of the reason for the wealth of talented artists who took to humorous and decorative work after the turn of the century was this profound distrust of 'Modern Art.' Bateman detested Matisse, and thought Picasso a trickster – not only that he used tricks in his paintings but that he was deliberately tricking the public into believing those paintings expressed anything serious or worthwhile. It infuriated him. He thought that 'in its search for freedom art has lost its way.'

> The subject has become of no real import, what matters are certain requirements in quality, the way the paint is laid on, texture of surface, rhythm of design, the harmonies of colour schemes; these are the things that count with connoisseurs and intellectuals. . . . A couple of beer bottles, a chamber pot, an ashcan . . . the move is towards the abstract when the object ceases to matter at all. What does count is an expression of the painter's mind . . . the public is invited to solve a riddle. If there is any sign of delusion, tension or other mental disturbance so much the better.[10]

Bateman had always despised 'intellectuals and connoisseurs,' and often satirized them in his cartoons, but the underlying reason for this scorn was anxiety about any form of self-questioning or analysis. He thought it wrong to poke about taking things to bits, a sort of silly game that interfered with the real point of a painting, its total effect, and destroyed its charm. The idea that an artist should be himself the subject of his painting, that the painting should reflect the mental state of the painter, he found abhorrent – which was oddly disingenuous of him, since he often introduced himself and his problems into his cartoons, fed off them, in a way, though possibly without quite realizing it. Psychiatrists were one of his pet hates.

In this he remained a kind of reactionary Edwardian all his life: caught in that period of transformation between Victorian self-satisfaction and twentieth-century self-questioning. Bateman, of course, was often far from self-satisfied, but he was in some ways an innocent, and seems hardly to have asked himself some very basic questions. He once wrote in a short unpublished and untitled essay, with an air of surprised discovery:

> . . . the question I want to ask is this: 'what is the true function of the Artist in everyday life and for that matter art in general?' I don't suppose many artists trouble to ask themselves about it even if the idea ever enters their heads.[11]

Such thoughts on this most self-conscious of all professions, to which he himself belonged, are a measure of his intellectual isolation – another aspect of his unworldliness and timidity. The question remained conspicuously unanswered.

12

AT FIRST SIGHT

On New Year's Eve 1925, something quite unexpected happened to Bateman. He fell in love. It was at the Chelsea Arts Ball, a fancy dress occasion, to which he went as a jockey, she as a Dutch girl. They were married the following September.

> I don't think at this stage in my life I believed in such a thing as 'Love at first sight' although I had previously done a drawing on the subject of its disturbing effect for *Punch*, but I quickly found I had been wrong, and we were married a few months afterwards.

It was something unexpected, not least to himself, and not only because he was now thirty-nine and had so far avoided any real relationship with a woman other than his mother, but because he had consistently looked upon marriage as a trap: a frightening combination of social pressure and the voraciousness of women, eager for the social standing a husband conferred. In his cartoons, married men were always beaten and battered into the shape the world and the wife demanded, and though this was a picture to some degree inherited from the traditional lore of marriage, in theatre, literature and the cartoon, it was more than a working stance.

His own parents' marriage offered a salutary lesson: a fine example of conflict masquerading as co-operation. Rows were frequent, and both he and his sister obviously suffered. He was devoted to his mother, but she was in some ways a fearsome example of her sex, strongly assertive and manipulative, and his timidity was perhaps a form of self-protective wisdom, learnt from close experience. In his sketch-books, her face deepens and squares over the years; his father's hides behind an ever-lengthening walrus moustache.

He had also watched his mother pushing his sister Phyllis to find a mate, with a determination that implied a deep desperation. First it had been his friend Frank Hart: Phyllis was packed off on a skiing holiday with them both (see chapter 8), and advised to seek him out alone and put her hand in his pocket. Frank Hart was not amused, and avoided any further intimacies, much to mother Bateman's chagrin. Phyllis remained unwed until 1923, the then miserable prospect of spinsterhood looming ever larger, but in that, her thirty-third year, having just settled in to the new house in Reigate, her mother discovered that living next door was a single middle-aged gentleman, Dr Arthur Porter, whose peaceful and solitary existence had not prepared him sufficiently to withstand any planned assault. While Bateman was away working – it was in 1923 that he went to America for the first time (see chapter 14) – Phyllis was frequently sent over to enlist Dr Porter's help with various domestic problems: matches to

Left:
'THE BACHELOR',
The Tatler, March 1921.

light a fire, or strong arms to move some furniture. Being extremely polite
and courteous, Dr Porter came rushing over to the two ladies, disadvan-
taged as they were with no man about the house. The demands upon him
steadily grew, until he was one day sent off with Phyllis to interview some
domestic help – an indelicate task for a single lady. When he returned from
his ride with Phyllis, he was confronted by her mother, who told him,
much to his surprise, that things could not possibly continue as they were,
that he had compromised her daughter by driving publicly abroad with
her, and that he must now do the only honourable thing, and marry her,
which he did. After their marriage, Phyllis became increasingly eccentric,
and hardly communicated with her brother. When Dr Porter died, some
years later, she spent her time going on long sea voyages with the money he
had left her, and suffered from a strange paranoia, imagining the pigeons
on the roof of her house – she had simply moved next door when she
married – were spies sent by some unknown power to keep watch upon
her. Even before she went into this long decline she was, at least,
emotionally fragile, and her mother's strength must have beaten upon her
like a hammer on thin metal.

So Bateman had within his own family two rather uninspiring
examples of the politics and practice of marriage. Yet this cannot entirely
account for the intensity of feeling in his cartoons on the subject. They are
wry, bitter and ironic, with a harsh edge, a cynicism perhaps partly
inherited from Caran d'Ache, but also a real bitterness entirely his own.

Opposite:
'THE PERFECT PET.'

To some degree he had forced this complex misogamy upon himself – although by nature an outsider, a man who sat apart and observed, he did not find the role entirely pleasant. Certainly it had contributed greatly to his unhappiness through his twenties and during the War. The intimacy of marriage was something of which he felt himself incapable, and therefore, in his own defence, and supported by close evidence, he made it inevitably horrible: he made sure he did not want what he thought he could not have. Before his marriage he had little experience of women, and never refers to anything of the sort in any of his writings, such as they remain. Indeed, it is true that beyond his mother and sister, and later his wife and daughters, hardly a figure of a woman appears in his sketch-books. It seems that he had not felt sufficiently relaxed before the sister, or mother, or wife of a friend to make a quick sketch of her. The one involvement he did have, during the War (see chapter 9) could hardly be described as such.

The relationships he did establish before his marriage – and it was never easy for him – were with men, and the deepest of these with William Caine. Here again there is some light thrown upon Bateman's attitude towards marriage; for Caine was a married man. In the years between the end of the First War and 1925, Caine and Bateman saw much of each other, going on frequent trips to the West Country, where they would find some remote inn on Dartmoor, or Exmoor, and walk, and paint and fish. Occasionally Caine would bring his wife along, but she was rather a city person, and did not share their love of the wild and the wet. Bateman resented her intrusion into their friendship, did not like her, and probably felt uneasy with her: they competed for Caine's attention. Caine was a kindly and sympathetic man, and it was at times difficult for him to balance their demands, though his first loyalty obviously lay with his wife. There survives part of a letter,[1] a reply from Caine to Bateman, who had appealed for help at a difficult moment. Caine was obliged to put him off, because he needed to attend to his wife, who was suffering from influenza.

What should have been the final nail in the structure of Bateman's misogamy was driven home in September 1925. Caine, who had for many years suffered from a weak heart, and was forbidden great exertion, collapsed and died in the arms of his wife while out dancing. It was a great tragedy to all his friends, but not unexpected. Bateman, quite wrongly, seems to have blamed Caine's wife.

Stephen Graham, in his Foreword to Caine's *The Glutton's Mirror*, published posthumously, in 1925, wrote of his life and death:

> William Caine . . . was one of the most versatile Bohemians of his time; a clever novelist, a genius in extravaganza, a gifted sentimental writer . . . a born humorist, he will find his place as such in any true estimate of our time.
>
> He had been for twelve years or more under sentence so to speak. The doctor stopped his pleasures one by one. . . . The one exercise which seemed to do him no harm was dancing, and in 1924, on the doctor's recommendation, he took up dancing and learnt all the new dances. . . . But he knew one day his heart would fail. . . . He came from a dance radiantly happy and died laughing. 'I have never enjoyed

anything so much in my life!' he said, and in the exuberance of exclamation his heart failed. But the smile did not fade.

A slightly bizarre picture, but one painted by a witness, and not to be doubted. Bateman, though, had nothing further to do with Caine's widow. Instead of inspiring him to rush off to the nearest monastery, however, Caine's death had just the opposite effect, perhaps shocking him into a sudden realization of his own solitude.

It is axiomatic that confirmed bachelors marry eventually. Certainly, for one so temperamentally unsuited to marriage, Bateman pursued the estate with a quiet determination that seems surprising until one knows

"I'm a faun," simpered Flack, "that's what I am—just a dear little sweet little fauny faun, and I've grown the dinkiest little pair of side whiskers you ever saw in your life—"

"And I'm a frightful success with the girls who make an *awful* fuss of me when I pay them a little attention—the *nice* girls you know, of course."

"Oh, yes, I play with paints and do the modern stunt and I've got a posh little hat and such a topping smock and all that, and I'm the last thing in ists and isms."

"And then I'm simply too priceless at costume and dressing up and all that sort of thing you know."

"Money? What *are* you talking about? Oh! you mean that silly stuff that people make so much fuss of and work for —I never bother about *that*—I get all I want from the old man—or the darling mater."

"And if they won't give it me, then I turn *horrid*, and *refuse* to gambol until they're *forced* to hand over."

"Which they always do, you bet—Oh, it's a' glorious life!" warbled Flack as he danced away on the sunbeams.

'THE FAUN',
London Opinion,
28 October 1922.

And one night when he was gambolling it happened that a real live tigress sprang at him and pulled him down, right in the open as it were.

Simply took him clean out of the centre of the herd and made him her prey.

"No," said Flack in after life, "I am no longer a faun—but I fawn."

that his wife-to-be was young, attractive, vivacious, and came from a world of which he had little real knowledge. Brenda Collison Wier was no suburban temptress. Her family lived in a large and lovely house at Langham, on the Essex–Suffolk border, and her father was a country gentleman, who devoted his time to the pursuits common to his class: sport and local society. She had never been to school, but was educated at home, with her sisters, by various governesses, as was often then the custom. This accounted for a certain wildness and independence of spirit which Bateman found disturbing yet interesting, at least during the early part of their relationship. Bateman was now, of course, a famous man, and fame has its own aura of attraction, but Brenda was certainly not overawed. She was used to men of reputation and to artists. Both A. J. Munnings – who lived nearby, at Deadham – and Wilson Steer were friends of her father, and visitors to their house. Munnings recalled him fondly in his autobiography as 'Dear Octavius.'[2]

Brenda's own circle of friends and acquaintances had been moving closer to Bateman's for some time, though they had never met before this New Year's Eve. Her mother's cousin, Harry Collison, a soldier, artist and anthroposophist, knew Bateman through the Chelsea Arts Club, of which he had been a long-standing member, and shared a house in Earls Court with Fred Pegram, the black-and-white artist and one of the original founder-members of the club, who had, of course, been close to Bateman, and most kind to him during the War. Brenda had often visited her cousin at the house.

Harry Collison was Brenda's escort at the ball, and it was he who introduced her to Bateman, not because he was an especially close friend but because he knew that she admired his work so much. Bateman's cartoons in *The Tatler* and *Punch* were much looked forward to at Langham, and greeted with roars of laughter. Brenda's mother had long said the two men she would most like to meet were Winston Churchill and H. M. Bateman. Both Brenda and her mother, of course, expected a man of coruscating wit, a vivid and humorous personality; they found him quite the reverse, which intrigued Brenda, but did little for her mother.

BRENDA COLLISON WIER.

It was slightly out of character for Bateman to go to a Chelsea Arts Club Ball at this time of his life. He had been involved in designing the décor for the club's Armistice Ball in 1919, and still spent time at the club itself, but by now, the eve of 1926, he was no longer given to such occasions of public frivolity. It was, of course, one of the great social events in London, and many otherwise dignified and solemn men took part, but Bateman strongly disliked such gatherings. Indeed, it was the last time he attended one: whenever his wife tried to persuade him to go again, he always refused. He had taken a box for his mother, and had probably gone to please her.

Bateman fell in love 'at first sight,' and quickly invited Brenda, with Harry Collison, to come and have lunch with him and his mother in Reigate, ostensibly to look through his work. They accepted, it was arranged, and they were met at the station by Bateman in his Minerva. He said not a word to his future wife, who thought him uncommonly rude, but put her in the back, seated 'uncle Harry' by his side, and drove home. He later admitted that he had been too shy to put her in the front with him, and too nervous to talk to her anyway.

It soon appeared that she made up for what he lacked in openness and gaiety, and he, some sixteen years older, touched her by his modesty, his lack of self-assurance, and his self-deprecation. They also soon discovered one very strong common bond, a deep love of the English countryside – especially the quieter, more unspoilt parts of it – and spent many hours going for long companionable walks in all weathers. Though they were to go regularly on holidays abroad, they always made sure to get away to the countryside as frequently as possible, and eventually bought a little cottage at All Cannings, near Devizes, in Wiltshire, which became a regular weekend retreat.

The courtship, however, did not pass into marriage without let or
hindrance. It was obvious from the start that there would be problems
with Bateman's mother, and Brenda's own parents did not take kindly to
the match. The reason for this was largely that they thought him far too
old, not only in years but also in outlook and behaviour. He did not really
fit in at Langham, and did not like the merry muscularity of some of their
friends. He thought much of the conversation rather shocking, and
retreated into his shell. Far from being the brilliantly funny man they had
expected, he seemed rather a prig and a spoilsport. There was also perhaps
a class problem which, had his personality been different, might never
have mattered.

But Brenda had quite made up her mind, and, despite opposition,
married Bateman, on September 29, 1926, at St Mark's Church, in
Hamilton Terrace, Maida Vale, London. Her parents did not attend the
wedding, but Brenda's brother, Terence Wier, gave her away, and Harry
Collison gave her a fine reception. The couple left immediately for a
honeymoon in Europe, travelling slowly by train through Austria and
Germany, and then on to Hungary, stopping at Budapest. In that most
romantic of cities, in search of the real Hungary, they dined in a tavern of
unimpeachable authenticity, while the band, in traditional costume,
played 'Tea for Two' through the evening.

Bateman had everything arranged for their return: they would live at
The Web, and his mother would move into a house he had bought for her
nearby. When they arrived home, they found mother Bateman standing on
the doorstep with arms folded. Her first words were 'You can't stay here.'
However, they managed to persuade her to go gently down the road, and
Brenda settled in to what was to be her home for the next eight years. With
sister Phyllis and husband next door, and mother Bateman not far off, the
atmosphere was a little close, but the couple often went away, sometimes
for Bateman's work – as in 1928, when he was commissioned by the
German magazine *Uhu*, and in 1932 to America (see chapter 14) – though
mostly for pleasure. They also soon had children: two daughters, Diana
and Monica, born in 1927 and 1929 respectively.

BATEMAN BY THORPE.

During this period, The Web was full and busy. Brenda was occupied
with the children, and Bateman was working hard, especially on his 'Man
Who . . .' series, (see next chapter) and on various advertising commissions
he had undertaken. It is true, however, that his rate of output began to
slow down perceptibly. The early part of 1925 had been immensely
productive, but in the year between Caine's death and his marriage
Bateman had published very little, possibly as a result of the emotional
disturbances of grief and love, or possibly, since his usual response to such
difficulties was to bury himself still deeper in his work, simply because he
needed a rest. He was also writing his book, *The Art of Drawing*, at this
time. His more leisurely output after his marriage reflected an altogether
less frantic approach. He was relaxed, and much less anxious about
himself and his health. A wife and children gave him, at first, a stability he
had not known before: he said he had never felt so well in his life. The
1920s, such mad and restless years for some, such tight and bitter times for
many others, closed for Bateman on a scene of contentment and domestic
happiness. It did not last.

13

THE MAN WHO...
AND OTHER
SITUATIONS

Although 'The Guardsman Who dropped It' marks the real beginning of the long series of 'Man Who . . .' cartoons that made Bateman so popular during the 1920s and 1930s, the idea had been brewing for some time. It was perhaps only public reaction to 'The Guardsman' that made him realize what a rich vein of material he had been tapping, less self-consciously, for years. Indeed, the publication of this cartoon marks out one of those distinctive moments in his career, like his 'going mad on paper,' in 1908, or his 'discovery' of the strip cartoon, in 1916, when he knew for certain he was on to something important. At these moments he was a real pioneer of the cartoon, and just as others had followed in his footsteps before, so, by the 1930s, there were a host of derivative 'Man Who . . .' cartoons, some of which appeared in *The Tatler* (such as those by Patrick Bellew) almost side by side with their progenitors. There was also a Dutchman whose reputation was based entirely on his imitations of Bateman's 'Man Who . . .' cartoons, feeble though these were by comparison.

There was, however, some dispute during the 1920s as to who in fact originated the 'Man Who . . .' idea. Fougasse (Kenneth Bird) also produced some 'Man Who . . .' cartoons at this time, and, according to Bevis Hillier, the editor of a collection of his work, his wife loyally ascribed the inspiration to him. 'His draughtsmanship did not compare in energy or invention with his chief *Punch* rival, H. M. Bateman, although Molly Bird stoutly maintains that it was Fougasse who first drew a cartoon in the series "The Man Who" which established Bateman's reputation, and that Bateman borrowed the idea.'[1] There was a kind of free trade arrangement among cartoonists, and they borrowed each other's ideas quite happily. The joke or the 'literature' of the cartoon especially was considered fair game – more perhaps than the style of drawing. Looking, for example, at the work of some of the London Sketch Club cartoonists in the period before the Great War one sees almost an in-joke of continual pastiche among them, and, of course, Bateman himself borrowed at various periods from Caran d'Ache and others. In this case, however, Bateman certainly did not borrow anything from Fougasse. The first of his drawings to use the 'Man Who . . .' caption appeared in one of his sketch-books as early as 1906, and the cartoon Bateman himself regarded as the original 'Man Who . . .,'

'The Missed Putt,' (though it lacked the 'Man Who . . .' caption) was
published in 1912. Even before this, he had published 'The Man Who
only wanted Two Halfpennies for a Penny' (1911), 'The Man Who never
used a Rest' (1911), and others too that contained all the elements of the
'Man Who . . .' situation.

'THE MAN WHO ONLY WANTED
TWO HALFPENNIES FOR
A PENNY.'

These cartoons appeared at a time when Kenneth Bird, though born in
the same year as Bateman, 1887, had not yet started to draw for
publication. He only came to it during the First War, while he lay in
hospital, horribly wounded, and realized he would have to find something
to do which would not overtax him physically. In fact, while he lay on his
back unable to do much more than read, he came to long for each new issue
of *Punch* and *The Tatler*, and especially for Bateman's cartoons in them. It

was very much the inspiration of Bateman, the way he showed what could be done with humorous drawing, that persuaded 'Fougasse' – French for the landmine by which he had been wounded – to try it himself. In later years Fougasse and Bateman became friends, and Fougasse stayed with him and Brenda at their home in Reigate, where he proved the most kind and delightful of guests.

Always conscious of his debt to others, Bateman was pleased rather than otherwise when his ideas were used. It was a compliment – though on one or two occasions his agent, A. E. Johnson, took it upon himself to write to other artists warning them that they were becoming too obviously imitative of his style. Fougasse, unlike some others, developed an entirely individual style of drawing, though he used some of the Bateman literature.[2]

Bateman's 'Man Who . . .' series – indeed most of his cartoons after 1922 – appeared exclusively in *Punch* and *The Tatler*, the second magazine devoting a full centre-page spread to Bateman, and making a tidy sum by selling prints of the cartoons at 10s.6d. a time.

Punch had, on the whole, become the magazine for Bateman's strip cartoons, and *The Tatler* the one for the single-incident drawings, though exactly why this should have been is difficult to see. Perhaps it was because the strip cartoons were largely black-and-white, which suited *Punch*, and the 'Man Who . . .' cartoons were in colour and suited the centre spread of *The Tatler*. There was also a curious gap in Bateman's association with *Punch*, between 1925 and 1930, just when the 'Man Who . . .' series was really getting under way, which helps to account for such a division.

The art editor of *Punch* at this time was Frank Reynolds, a fellow cartoonist, and friend and admirer of Bateman, so there was almost certainly no policy decision to exclude him. It was most probably due to a demand by Bateman for more money: *Punch* was notoriously mean, and still took the attitude that the honour of being asked to contribute was really reward enough. A. A. Milne, for instance, remembered a very frosty, almost shocked reception to his request for a slightly larger emolument,[3] and Bateman, who could now command a considerable fee, was always keen to get as much as he could for his work. By 1925, anyway, *Punch* seems to have agreed to his terms, realizing the anomaly in Britain's leading humorous magazine not featuring the work of Britain's leading humorous artist, and the renewed association continued until Bateman's retirement from the scene.

The majority of the 'Man Who . . .' cartoons describe some terrible social misdemeanour, some offence against accepted behaviour and custom. They fall into two broad categories: either the protagonist, or offender, is shown recoiling in horror from his action and the attention focused upon it, or he carries blithely on, innocent of the outrage he has perpetrated, and the world's indignant roar. They also contain those repeated formulaic descriptions of consternation, anger or disgust, such as eyeballs popping right out of their sockets, contorted bodies, bodies prone or airborne, which became hallmarks of the Bateman cartoon.

The characters are usually drawn from the fashionable middle classes, and the cartoons not only single out for ridicule and scrutiny the individual who has committed the solecism but, perhaps more forcibly, the society

A UNIQUE COLLECTION OF PICTURES

BY
H. M. BATEMAN

"Very Well Meant"

"The Man who Bid Half-a-Guinea at Tattersall's"

"The Guardsman who Dropped It"

Specially mounted and printed copies in colour of this famous series of pictures can now be obtained.

Size of work of each picture 14 ins. by 10 ins., on plate sunk mounts 25 ins. by 20 ins.

"The Favourite Wins"

Copies of each picture
10/6 each.

Proofs, signed by the Artist, of each
20/= each.
Postage 6d. extra.

"The Man who Missed the Ball on the First Tee at St. Andrews"

"The Man who Lit His Cigar before the Royal Toast"

"The Umpire who Confessed He wasn't Looking"

"Figaro Chez Lui"

"The Girl who Ordered a Glass of Milk at the Café Royal"

An
Ideal Gift

Orders with Remittance to be sent to—

"The Discovery of a Dandelion on the Centre Court at Wimbledon"

DEPT. E, "THE TATLER," 346, STRAND, LONDON, W.C.2

'THE MAID WHO WAS BUT
HUMAN',
Punch, 13 December 1922.

that condemns it. The smallest deviation from the accepted norm of behaviour could disturb the formal calm of polite society; the more one looks at Bateman's cartoons the more one feels that, despite his conservatism, his sympathies lay not with the offended but with the offender and the offence. There is also a sympathy for the underdog, the little man, the object of scorn.

Although the cartoons seem at times to lend weight to George Orwell's description of England in the 1930s as a 'land of snobbery and privilege ruled over by the old and silly,' they were immensely popular, and not only, as Bateman himself suggested, because of the enjoyment felt at another's discomfiture. People recognized the reality behind the exaggeration. Bateman even gave them a new and less awkward way of covering their embarrassment, and such predicaments as he described became 'real Bateman situations.' Many of his cartoons focused on classic social arenas, like the party, the club, the game and, above all, the meal table. It was here that his vision of a society obsessed by the done thing, and fraught with potential disaster at every gathering, was most consistent. He returned time and again to the formal dinner as a set piece for his confrontations.

Mealtimes and dinner parties had always excited Bateman's amusement and attention – one remembers those Edwardian cartoons on food and drink, and other later ones like 'The Plum that took a Wrong Turning' – but there was a special sense in which, during the 1920s and 1930s, the dinner, with its rigid form but varied composition, became for him what the sonnet had been to Elizabethan poets: a ready-made vehicle, capable of infinite variation and refinement, with its subject matter, its terms, its nuances immediately recognizable to its public. In his last *Forsyte Saga* volume, Galsworthy wrote – and one feels he had just put down a copy of *Punch* or *The Tatler* – 'That the most pregnant function of human life is the meal, will be admitted by all who take part in these recurrent crises. The impossibility of getting down from the table renders it the most formidable of human activities among people civilized to the point of swallowing not only their food but their feelings.'[4]

In middle-class society during the 'roaring Twenties,' manners and morals had become less constraining, but the trend toward informality met with considerable resistance. In fact those suggestions during the early 1920s that society was breaking up, that its traditional gestures had become redundant, gave way in the 1930s to a sense of social order restored: the progressiveness and promiscuity of the Twenties became a thing of the past. Despite unrest, strikes, the 'Bolshevik Menace,' many felt that another Golden Age was dawning – a period of peace, calm and stability, like the Victorian age they still remembered with a sense of loss. Galsworthy could write, 'Revolution? There never was a time when it had less chance.'[5] It was against such a background, where old customs still prevailed, that the subject of a man lighting his cigar before the Royal Toast could be effectively funny. Indeed, it remains so today, or is at least recognizable as such, because, despite all the changes of the past sixty years, Britain is still a stiffly class-conscious society, in which all the forms and apparel of class still matter, and are immediately and vividly descriptive. The man in the cartoon is a bounder, betraying his stiff white shirt and his host's invitation.

While Bateman exploited and made fun of the tension between the expectation of the done thing and the actuality of the thing definitely not done, others were concerned to reinforce the code of manners upon which their society was based and could founder. In 1922, in New York, Emily Post's book, *Etiquette*, was published: it went on to sell over four million copies. It was the book people referred to if they wished to know how to introduce an ex-President of the United States or whether frock coats were acceptable on board a steamer. More than this, however, it was an illuminating essay on the aspirations of middle-class society, and reads now like a social history of the times. Emily Post's characters could have been Bateman characters – Richand Vulgar, Mrs Worldly, the Smartlys, the Oldnames, the Lovejoys – and her passages on, for example, the Bore, the Offence of Pretentiousness, the Theatre Pest, could have served as captions to Bateman cartoons. She caught hold of and analyzed the affront that Bateman's cartoons celebrate, for the heart and theme of her book is the unacceptability of public display, or of any form of odd or aberrant behaviour by which one might attract attention.

> Do not attract attention to yourself in public. This is one of the fundamental rules of good breeding. Shun conspicuous manners, conspicuous clothes, a loud voice, staring at people, knocking into them, talking across them. In a word, do not attract attention to yourself. Do not expose your private affairs, feelings or innermost thoughts in public. You are knocking down the walls of your own house when you do.

The popularity of Emily Post's book and of Bateman's cartoons shows how topical their subject was: to have a relevant comedy of manners it is first

'The Guest Who Called the Foie Gras Potted Meat', *The Tatler*.

necessary to have an acknowledged, not to say rigid, code of manners to mock. The 'Man Who . . .' cartoons, however, do not only mock or echo the concerns of society, they also witness a more personal involvement with the subject than such seemingly detached comments would suggest. Bateman was undoubtedly fascinated by the awkward moment. It is one of the paradoxes of his personality that, reticent and timid though he was, shrinking away from self-revelation, he could at times bring attention upon himself in the most brazen way.

He could plunge himself and others into situations which would have brought a cold sweat on to the brow of a far less sensitive man – and, as one might have expected, these problems seemed often to arise at a dinner party. Once, he and his wife were invited by her cousin, Harry Collison, to a grand formal dinner given by the Grocers Company in London: he was Master that year. As they were going in to dinner with all the other guests, having come up from Reigate specially for the evening, Bateman suddenly started to say in a noticeable fashion that he did not want to go inside, that he did not feel like it after all. When his wife protested, he tried to make her promise they would leave no later than ten o'clock. This she declined to do, and eventually they went in to dinner in some confusion. It was a special occasion, a Ladies Night, and, as was the custom, the lady guests all sat upstairs with the present Master and past Masters. During the meal, Brenda was enjoying herself, and did not pay much attention to her husband. Then, at just after ten o'clock, halfway through a speech by Lord Astor, she looked towards her husband's place and found him gone. She sat through the rest of the dinner acutely anxious lest her cousin, their

Above:
'THE DIRT-TRACK RIDER WHO APPEARED IN ROTTEN ROW', *The Tatler*.

Opposite Above:
'THE MAN WHO LIT HIS CIGAR BEFORE THE ROYAL TOAST', *The Tatler*.

Opposite Below:
'THE MAN WHO THREW A SNOWBALL AT ST MORITZ', *The Tatler*.

host, or any of their other acquaintances had noticed he was missing, and in some trepidation about the scene that would follow. But Bateman, obviously, was not in the least concerned for her feelings, nor did he care what his host might think of him. At the end of the evening, Brenda went off to look for him, and eventually found him lurking in one of the lifts in a black mood. The journey back to Reigate was extremely unpleasant.

One has admiration for someone capable of leaving a dinner like that when he feels like it, in the middle of Lord Astor's speech – indeed he disproved Galsworthy's remark about the 'impossibility of getting down from the table.' This, however, was no gay impulsiveness, but rather a morbid action which brought only ill-temper in its wake. Here was Bateman as 'The Man Who left the City Dinner during the Guest of Honour's Speech,' and as such he might perhaps have recognized a certain humour in the situation. But he could not. He was furious. Of course, he always expected his wife to obey him implicitly, no matter how unreasonably, and any suspicion of disobedience provoked increasing stubbornness.

There is, too, a sense in which the 'Man Who . . .' cartoons were a projection of a perverse impishness in Bateman's character. Under his quiet exterior there hid a mischievous desire to disturb the peace, which found expression in such cartoons as 'The Dirt-Track Rider who appeared in Rotten Row,' good-humoured and funny, or 'The Man Who threw a Snowball at St Moritz,' where his description of self-righteous indignation is so heavy that it becomes difficult to contemplate. This was often the case in drawings which included crowds jeering, laughing or looking at one person, singled out for whatever reason. Bateman himself hated people coming round him while he worked, sketching outside in some public place, and it took a great effort of will for him not to shout at any such inquisitive gathering, and tell the people all to go away and mind their own business. He felt at times an uneasiness – something almost sinister – in the behaviour of people *en masse*. Such a feeling comes through strongly in a cartoon like 'The Admission' – really another 'Man Who . . .' cartoon ('The Man Who admitted he was Guilty') in everything but title. All the laughing faces appear at first too insensitive, too gross, but gradually the picture takes hold. Bateman had seen something real and rather horrible.

If the heart of such a cartoon was based on reality, its composition has obviously been stage-managed. Here again is that theatricality characteristic of so much of Bateman's work: the exaggerated expressions, the large gestures, the melodrama. The cartoons are often about some confrontation between an individual and his audience, and sometimes his offenders have a little space around them, as though spotlit on a stage, all suggestive of those months he spent as the theatre artist for *The Sketch*. As with those earlier drawings, which he strove to bring to life through a physical understanding of emotion, so these 'Man Who . . .' cartoons convey great physical involvement. One does, of course, react to awkwardness and embarrassment in a very physical way: by shrinking away, cringing, curling up, or hiding one's face in one's hands. These expressions are also used to describe a feeling metaphorically – as in 'I felt so small.' Bateman took them literally, translating a verbal into a visual image – a wonderfully simple idea.

Opposite:
'THE LATE ARRIVALS',
The Tatler, 3 December 1922.

'There are no greater pests than those who come back after the curtain has gone up and temporarily snuff out the view of everyone behind, as well as annoy those who are obliged to stand up to let them by.'
Emily Post, *Etiquette*.

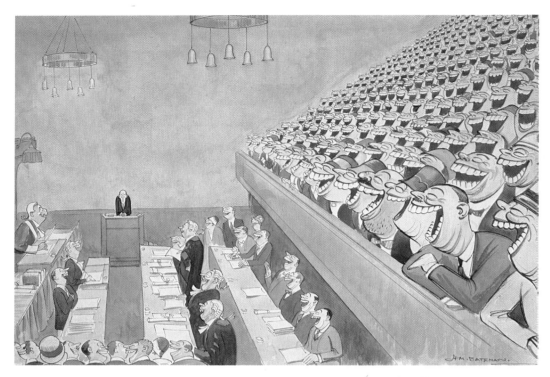

Above:
'THE MANNEQUIN WHO MADE THE MOST OF IT',
The Tatler, October 1935.
A movement towards stylization.

Right:
SAVOY, LONDON, 1905.
It did not take long for the advertisers
to recognize a good idea.

Above Left:
'THE ADMISSION',
The Tatler, 29 April 1931.

Left:
'THE GIGOLO WHO REFUSED TO
DANCE',
The Tatler, 1936.
The crudeness was intentional and could
add to a cartoon which sought to impart
a feeling of revulsion or loathing.

The footmen who couldn't resist it

SAVOY

LONDON
1925

Inspired though the idea for the 'Man Who . . .' cartoons was, it set an invidious trap for its creator. The trouble was that whereas other of his 'discoveries,' like the strip cartoon, had been technical devices, or innovations in drawing style, this was a formula, capable of infinite repetition, but still inescapably a formula, which constrained all his creative ideas into a predetermined pattern. By the 1930s, he was losing interest, much of his drawing now losing the force of originality, and becoming cruder – though sometimes the crudeness was intentional, and could add to a cartoon which sought to impart a feeling of revulsion or loathing.

The problem was success itself, the continuing demand for these cartoons, the popularity, the financial security. He dared not stop. Many years later, he wrote:

> The roads to success are cluttered up with tales of breakdowns, engine failures, bad luck stories, the unknown odds, and other excuses – the debris of failure . . . people continue to arrive and some make lasting stays, whilst for others their sojourn is a good deal briefer, a year or two, a month or two before they find themselves returned to outer darkness.[6]

He goes on to say that once a reputation has been achieved it becomes increasingly difficult to produce any innovation, for 'any change would not be understood. When a certain pitch has been reached, worldly wisdom prompts a policy of "safety first".'

This was undoubtedly part of the process when Bateman found himself stuck in the 'Man Who . . .' series, but there was also his deliberate decision to concentrate more on 'serious' painting – to become a painter – which occupied him from the 1930s until his death. In many ways it is a great pity that he did not persevere as a cartoonist, because by the mid-1930s he was beginning to show that his work was again capable of radical change and innovation after all. One must conclude that other things became more important to him. The change that some of his later work shows is a movement towards simplicity and stylization. His cartoons became more an arrangement of shapes and lines than an attempt to characterize. People were no longer types, but abstractions. This could have been a most fertile field to cultivate, an interesting and amusing road to explore, but, unfortunately, it was not to be.

The 'Man Who . . .' did not only become familiar to the public through the pages of *Punch* and *The Tatler*: Bateman's creations looked out at them from newspapers, from brochures and calendars, and from hoardings. It did not take long for the advertisers to recognize a good idea, and soon dozens of products were recommended on the grounds of their wonderful benefit to the Man Who bought them or the dire consequences awaiting the Man Who did not. Beer, cigarettes, radios, radio valves, shavers, windows, holidays, restaurants, philanthropic societies, Christmas gifts, paint, motor cars, mustard, clothes, tonics and conditioners for livestock, the list goes on. Indeed, 'Man Who . . .' cartoons, and imitations of 'Man Who . . .' cartoons are still being used today to sell various products: one can see them in the Sunday magazines or on the walls of the London Underground, helping to liven up those dreary intestinal tubes.

'COCKTAIL FACE' –
'THE NEW FASHIONABLE DISEASE.'

A LOT of people have been talking about this new poster drawn by the famous humorous artist H. M. Bateman.

The lesson it conveys is very simple: Mustard is an *important* part of every meal at which meat is eaten and not just a condiment.

In fact, it is remarkable how much that little dab of Colman's Mustard does, not only to increase your enjoyment but still more to improve your digestion. *Meat needs Mustard.* See that your Mustard is freshly made.

COLMAN'S MUSTARD advertisement.

Already by the early years of the twentieth century advertisement had become a major force, a controller and conditioner of life, and taste. H. G. Wells has one of his characters in *Tono Bungay* (a fraudulent tonic) say:

'Advertisement has revolutionized trade and industry; it is going to revolutionize the world. The old merchant used to tote about commodities; the new one creates values. Doesn't need to tote. He takes something that isn't worth anything – or something that isn't particularly worth anything – and he makes it worth something. He takes mustard that is just like anybody else's mustard and he goes about saying, shouting, singing, chalking on walls, writing inside people's books, putting it everywhere, "Smith's Mustard is Best!" and behold it is the Best.'

Although it was not until the 1920s, and the 'Man Who . . .' series, that Bateman became, for the advertiser, someone to fight over, he, like other leading cartoonists, such as Heath Robinson, had become involved in advertising at a much earlier date. His first ever commission had been in 1904 (see chapter 2), and over the succeeding years he took up others. Perhaps the most interesting of these early advertisements was the one produced by the Nickeloid Electrotype Company: interesting because it shows Bateman being used to advertise – and himself using – the newest developments in colour reproduction in books and magazines.

It was, however, later, and in association with the great consumer market rather than the specialized industrial one, that Bateman's advertisements became best known. Most insistent of all was the series of 'Man Who . . .' advertisements he produced for Kensitas cigarettes: smoking Kensitas, the mild cigarette, would prevent those disastrous fits of coughing which a rougher tobacco could induce. He created forty or more cartoons on the theme of 'The Man Who coughed at the First Night,' 'The Man Who coughed during the Billiard Match,' 'The Man Who coughed at the Board Meeting,' and so on. He also did many advertisements for Guinness, and was summoned abroad on various commissions – once to Germany, in 1926, and to America, for Lucky Strike cigarettes, in 1932 (see next chapter).

In these days of great sophistication in advertising, Bateman's contributions seem genial, uncomplicated, almost naïve, but, judging by the number of commissions he received, they were certainly deemed effective. Just the association of his name with a product was enough to focus public attention upon it, and if he himself ever needed a little reassurance, a little fillip for his ego, he could stroll along the Embankment, by the Thames, in London, and look up at his huge neon advertisement for the *News Chronicle*, over 108 ft. long, and 15 ft. high, and reflect that almost everyone who passed would recognize it for a Bateman.

ADVERTISEMENT
for the Nickeloid
Electrotype Company.

Reproduced from H. M. Bateman's poster sketch advertising that successful play

— *"The Glad Eye"* —

AN example of Three Colour letter-press printing produced by our "Ultimatt" process, which gives the effect of original painting on hand-made paper without loss of detail or colour values. Quotations gladly given on request.

The
NICKELOID ELECTROTYPE CO., LTD.
10 NEW STREET HILL, LONDON, E.C.4.

14
AMERICAN EXPRESSIONS

Bateman visited America three times: first, in 1923, out of curiosity, then with his wife, in 1932, and later, and more briefly, during his world trip, in 1938. His reputation had preceeded him some time before he set foot on American soil, and in the years between the end of the Great War and his visit in 1923 a number of his cartoons were copyrighted in the U.S.A., appearing there before being published in England. His work was also discussed in various magazines and newspapers in the States, and his 1921 exhibition at the Leicester Galleries was noted and praised as it had been in England. That august journal the Boston *Christian Science Monitor*, devoting, as did many of the newspapers of the time, what seems by today's standards an extravagant amount of space to artistic matters, published a review in 1921 entitled, 'Bateman on his Pegasus of Humour.'

> London, England – Two years ago when Mr Bateman held an exhibition of his drawings a queue had to be formed of the crowds of visitors to see them. At the present exhibition much the same thing happens. People flock round some special favourite and laugh. They laugh with that same irresponsible unconsciousness with which children laugh. Humour such as Mr Bateman's compels this. His drawing is swift, discarding everything but the essential point he wishes to make. He seems to laugh and the line of the drawing laughs. It is here that he is supreme in his own way. For almost every one of the drawings is a humorous thing quite apart from the story it has to tell.[1]

Of the cartoons that first appeared in America only a few had any direct reference to particularly American topics, and those were not among his best work. The arrangement to publish there seems to have been made between A. E. Johnson, Bateman's agent, who was always enterprising in exporting the best artists on his books to the Continent and America, and, for some reason, certainly financial, *London Opinion*, which published almost exclusively the cartoons which first appeared in America.

Bateman was, therefore, quite well known in the U.S.A. before 1923, and though he was supposed to be there on a holiday it was not long before he found himself with commissions to fulfil.

> ... it was not long after I arrived – it seemed only a matter of a few minutes – before unexpected people made contact with me, and I found myself caught up in the world of publishing similar to the one with which I was familiar in England and had just left behind. Before my first morning in New York had passed I had undertaken to do a

series of drawings showing my reactions to and impressions of American life. Americans I found were sensitive people, always anxious to find out what a visitor from another country thought about their way of doing things, even though the visitor happened to be no more than a humorous artist.[2]

Ever after impressed by the speed and enthusiasm which marked his transactions there, he found the American eagerness for business surprising, at first, and stimulating. He had been given a letter of introduction to the Salmagundi Club, in New York, an arts club rather like the Savage or the Chelsea Arts in London, with which it was affiliated, and 'within half an hour of getting installed, the telephone in my bedroom began to ring, and on answering I found that I was being rung up by the office of *Life*.'[3]

Life, now defunct, was then the leading humorous magazine in America, and its editor, Dana Gibson, perhaps the country's best known humorous artist. Bateman had probably already met him in England, where he had worked for some time, many of his cartoons appearing in *London Opinion* and *Punch*. Indeed *Life* was not unlike *Punch*: it promoted the same kind of decorous humour, took itself rather seriously, and was most self-consciously a 'voice.' In January 1923, the magazine celebrated its fortieth anniversary, and announced itself thus:

> The world, shaken by the impact of the Great War, has not yet achieved the Great Peace for which she fought. Irishmen are killing Irishmen in the same genial wholehearted fashion in which they killed the hated Sassenachs. Turks are disposing of vast numbers of Christians, while we shake our heads and murmur faint admonishments. France has a heart full of bitterness, Germany is teaching us the gentle art of defalcation. America holds the purse strings of the world and is doing her best, with the help of a prohibitive tariff, to keep her neighbours poor. England, never too proud to fight, and always too proud to owe, is crushing herself with taxes to pay us interest on her debt. And it is up to the forty-year-old *Life* to quicken our spirits and make us laugh in the face of circumstance.

To which end *Life* published some thirteen full-page Bateman cartoons between June and September 1923. A few – those not peculiarly American – were later reproduced in England, but most of them were inspired by New York, and were never seen outside the pages of *Life*.

Despite the depression, despite prohibition – perhaps even partly because of it – New York was the great dynamic, exciting city of the Twenties, and everybody wanted to know about it. On his return to England, Bateman was asked by the *Pall Mall* magazine to contribute an article on his experiences there – and it is from this year that he appears in his part-time role of occasional journalist: an occupation of which he could undoubtedly have made a career, and to which he devoted more and more time as the years went by. He wrote very much in the current magazine idiom – lightheartedly and with exuberance – and in a style which gave no hint of the shy, anxious and often melancholy man who sometimes so interestingly revealed himself in the most powerful of his cartoons. The

A NEW YORK COP DIRECTING
TRAFFIC.

article he wrote, and illustrated, for the *Pall Mall* was called simply 'What I Thought of New York.'

New York is all right, all right. It is a mighty fine place, and almost unexpectedly comes up to expectations. I say almost unexpectedly, because, like the majority of people, I am in the habit of finding that the reality is seldom equal to the anticipation. But with New York that is all different: if it does not entirely equal anticipation in all details, it more than makes up with interest in other ways. The buildings really are tall, the people really are in an appalling hurry, the noises and counter-noises really are ear-splitting, the elevators elevate, and having descended, again elevate unceasingly, whilst everything is pulsating with an energy and activity which is catching. You are whirled up, and before you have time to think about it you are running, pushing, and fighting for your dear life with the best of them.

The first and foremost characteristic of the city and its mode of life is speed. This is impressed upon you immediately on arrival. The rapidity with which I found the contents of my portmanteaux emptied upon the quay by the customs official, in his effort to make good and so justify his existence, was amazing, and to a slow-witted Briton, who had given considerable forethought to his outfit and some hours to carefully packing the same, it came with a real surprise to see the whole mass displayed upon the ground within the twinkling of an eye, by one who had only just made my acquaintance. An understanding having at length been come to, I was seized with the spirit of hustle and made record time in restoring the various items to their receptacles. These were then hurried along a moving platform to the street, myself racing meanwhile to keep in touch with them, and thrown into a salmon-pink taxicab, which hurtled to the hotel. I was ejected, checked in, rushed into the elevator, shot sky high, and installed.

Looking down from the immense height of the bedroom window, the street below appears to be full of tiny moving objects, which, if your eyesight is good enough, you will recognize as human beings and their motor-cars. . . .

It is interesting to note that the front of every motor is fitted with a simple form of buffer, which they tell me is intended to protect the headlights and front of the car from being knocked about in the press of traffic – but my own private opinion is that it is really designed to deal with the pedestrian who is not quick enough to dodge it successfully. I assume this to be a modern development of the old-fashioned cow-catcher, and is intended to act in the same way. Now the air of New York is noted for its stimulating properties, but I am inclined to think, on consideration, that the real truth of the matter lies in the fact that with a motor traffic so prodigious, the pedestrian is everlastingly being forced to activity in order to avoid extinction, and in this way the amount of exercise he unwittingly takes keeps him fit and in the best possible condition. If by any conceivable chance the traffic of New York could be done away with or in any way lessened, I should not be surprised to find that the result would be a general lowering of the present excellent standard of health and physical

fitness all round. In spite of the tonic effect of this ceaseless activity, the wear and tear upon the system must not be overlooked, and in addition to the ordinary meals of the day, the body appears to demand some other form of sustenance, in order to help meet the demands made upon it. The peanut and ice-cream appear to furnish all that is required in this way, if I may judge by the quantities of both commodities which are consumed.[4]

Bateman obviously enjoyed the excitement and bustle of 'little old New York,' and, in his autobiography, wrote admiringly of the 'American system,' which, he said, 'differs somewhat from ours in that if a man is proving useful in any direction he is helped considerably – in order, no doubt, that he may probably prove still more useful – whereas in England if anyone shows promise the tendency is to apply handicaps, and yet more handicaps for him to carry before he finally succeeds in establishing himself on secure ground.'

This first trip to America was not all bustle and business, however, for he went off on his own to South Carolina, and stayed near Charleston, on an old cotton plantation, where he spent a week sketching the countryside and its black inhabitants.

Bateman's attitude towards black Americans was imperial, but his experience of them was slight, as many another Englishman's would then have been, based entirely upon his devotion to the music hall and variety shows in which they appeared as singers and dancers, purveyors of ragtime, hootchy-koo, the Charleston, and other such delights. It was, then, a long-standing and frank curiosity which impelled him towards South Carolina, and if his opinions were bigoted, his drawings were full of sympathy and charm.

Remembering his time there, he wrote in his autobiography that he went:

> . . . right among the niggers, of whom there were many families living in wooden shacks round about the old Southern house in which I stayed. I must confess to being fascinated by niggers and I started to make a lot of sketches of them, finding them good sitters and satisfied with a few cents payment. They seemed to like being drawn, and for two or three days I had all the models I needed, many of them coming to offer themselves for the job. But suddenly the flow ceased, and if I saw a nigger at all it was nothing more than his coat tails disappearing behind a tree or slinking round to the back of the house whenever I approached.
>
> It was surprising after the keenness they had first shown and I asked the 'boss' of the place if he could explain what had happened to bring about the sudden change.
>
> The next day he gave me the reason. Niggers are childlike and notoriously vain, and at first they were flattered and only too ready to pose. But they are also born thieves, and in the evenings they had been putting their heads together as to why I was so anxious to get their likenesses on paper, and it had suddenly occurred to them that I might be a detective or spy of some sort, who would print all their portraits in a *Police Gazette* for future reference.

SKETCH OF AMERICAN BLACK
from sketch-book.

Bateman's second visit to America was in 1932, when he went, taking his wife, Brenda, with him, on a commission for a series of advertisements for the American Tobacco Company. Lucky Strike cigarettes had earned George Hill a fortune, and it was with this great baron of the business world that Bateman at first stayed, in baroque magnificence, in a house which 'resembled a palace from the Arabian Nights.' George Hill, a kind and courteous man, treated Bateman as an important person, which he enjoyed, and made sure that the couple had everything they could wish for. When the time came for them to go off round the States so that Bateman could get some 'background' for his drawings, they were provided with first-class train tickets and hotel accommodation.[5]

Before they left on their tour, however, they stayed in New York at one of the grandest hotels in the city, and Bateman, ever watchful for the peculiar and different, recorded his time there in an unpublished book, called *Homes from Home*.

On arrival at New York I went to the Waldorf Astoria and settled in there for the better part of a fortnight. It was an experience I would not have missed for anything. I had an introduction to one of the managers of the Waldorf from a friend of mine, a director of our Savoy Hotel in London, and this no doubt helped to make easy my entrance into what at first appeared as a strange rather fantastic world, apart from a little argument at first on the subject of height.

Unlike England, where the first or second-floor bedrooms are considered the best and most convenient, in America the choicest rooms and apartments are situated at the top, for reasons of more light, airiness and quiet – the last named feature in particular. The higher you go the more of the amenities you expect to enjoy, and the more you expect to have to pay for them. ... I do not like height. It does not

appeal to me. I am one of those people who would rather be on or near the ground floor. . . .

Eventually they fixed me up with a delightful room on the seventh floor, which was as high as I would go, and as high up as anything I subsequently engaged on my round trip through the States that followed. Whether my insistence on these less elevated rooms caused any lowering in appraisal of my social and financial status among the staffs of the many reception desks encountered on this tour, I don't know. At the Waldorf Astoria I got a good insight into American ways and a foretaste, on an elevated level perhaps, of what it would be like further on. With an hour to spare in the great entrance hall it would be a very obtuse person who could not extract a lot of information from watching the swarming crowds and the various activities taking place around him, and much entertainment to boot. A lot more everyday business was done there than in comparable English and European hotels, concerned more with purely residential arrangements. And then America has always been a more democratic country than England. Practically every grade or class of American citizen, conforming to a decent standard of appearance and manners, would at some time appear there, going about their affairs. It was like a microcosm of the country's life, a world within a world. My English sense of humour and reserve was tickled by the way in which certain things were done; for example the uniforms – I would rather describe them as costumes – of the bell boys, hall porters and other attendants were so bright and so varied that the general scene resembled a musical comedy or revue. As to the appointments of the rooms there was little that had not been thought of. At that time prohibition was still in force, which meant that everywhere a lot of drinking went on secretly. Most men and plenty of women too carried a flask or had a bottle of liquor somewhere in their baggage, and in many hotel bedrooms a small pocket corkscrew would be found hanging ready for use with the name of the establishment engraved on it. I collected several of these as souvenirs.

The period which covers Bateman's three trips to America was also that of national prohibition, which lasted from 1919 until 1933. Heralded as the 'greatest social experiment of modern times,' prohibition gave rise to many absurdities, and Bateman, who was not a drinking man, but, like a boy at school, obviously got a perverse delight out of a surreptitious tipple, made several comic drawings on the subject.

The years of prohibition were notoriously violent, and there was a certain tension in the big cities the Batemans visited, made all the more noticeable by the public anger over the kidnapping and murder of the Lindbergh baby, which occurred while they were there. More tangible evidence was the gun in the glove pocket of the car in which the chauffeur, provided by George Hill, would drive them about town. Once in San Francisco, on a sightseeing tour with an American friend, a cousin of Damon Runyon, they saw two bootleggers fighting in the street, and one man was shot dead in front of them. Brenda was told brusquely not to look, for fear of her being followed and shot as a witness. Bateman himself was

Opposite:
'TRUE AMERICAN HOSPITALITY.'

already looking away, embarrassed by the scene. It was odd that he who could so vividly analyze, describe, and make fun of the embarrassing situation, not only recognized it so quickly but was so affected by it – though this, of course, was a rather more dramatic predicament than he was used to. It was not that he was physically afraid, but that he could not bear the fuss that involvement in this or many other situations would bring – part of the inconsistency of his temperament, since he sometimes relished moments of obtrusion. He shrank away, muttering to Brenda that she should not interfere.

The same thing was to happen, less dramatically, later on their tour, when they went to watch a golf match in New Orleans. Bateman was, of course, a player of the game, and devoted many cartoons to it; and this match was an important one, with famous men competing. At one point, the great Walter Hagen hit a mighty drive, and the ball was lost to sight. From where they were standing, however, the Batemans could see that it had rolled into a ditch. Suddenly, from behind a hedge, there popped up a little coloured boy who swooped down upon the ball, put it into his mouth, and was gone in a flash. After a moment of confusion and then laughter, Brenda, thinking it not quite fair, decided she should tell someone what she had seen. Bateman would have none of it, and forebade her to do so.

Brenda's American education was extensive, and not merely confined to the sights: some of those eccentricities of personality which her husband revealed at this time did not promise too well for their future. His parsimony, for instance, was becoming extreme and unreal; as the best-paid cartoonist in England he had no need to count his pennies, yet he persistently refused to tip anybody, even at the Waldorf Astoria, where he was staying free of charge, causing great embarrassment to his wife and any company they might have. The reasons for this meanness were many, and had much to do with his family background, his natural carefulness, and his relationship with the Inland Revenue. From these years until the end of his life, however, it appeared as one of the most noticeable aspects of his character. In New York, while Bateman was working, his wife spent some time window-shopping, and eventually went into Saks, the famous Fifth Avenue department store, where she was served by a splendid Russian prince, who was a salesman there, and she bought three pairs of shoes. Bateman was absolutely furious, and made her take all but one pair back. He seemed to derive a curious pleasure from such situations.

Yet the visit was on the whole much more enjoyable than all this would suggest. They travelled extensively, and, as well as New York, San Francisco, and New Orleans, went to Chicago, and to Hollywood, where they stayed for a time, watched some films being made, and visited the Walt Disney studios.

This was particularly interesting to Bateman: he had created a series of drawings – more than eight hundred, in fact – for an animated cartoon, 'long before Walt Disney's name was ever heard of.' Unfortunately these drawings are lost to us now, but his love of the cinema, of the cartoon film *Felix the Cat*, and of Charlie Chaplin, whose signed photograph he possessed, though he possessed no other such token, add substance to his claim. More weighty, though, is evidence of the cartoons themselves, especially the strip cartoons he published in *Punch* and *The Tatler* such as

'THE ONE-NOTE MAN' – I.

'The One-Note Man' – II.

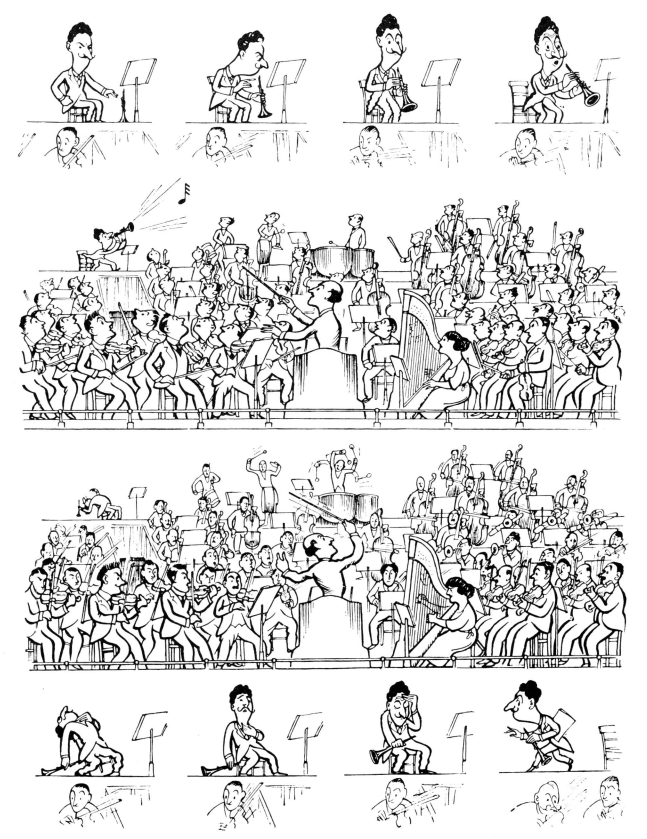

'THE ONE-NOTE MAN' – III.

'THE ONE-NOTE MAN' – IV,
Punch, 14 December 1921.

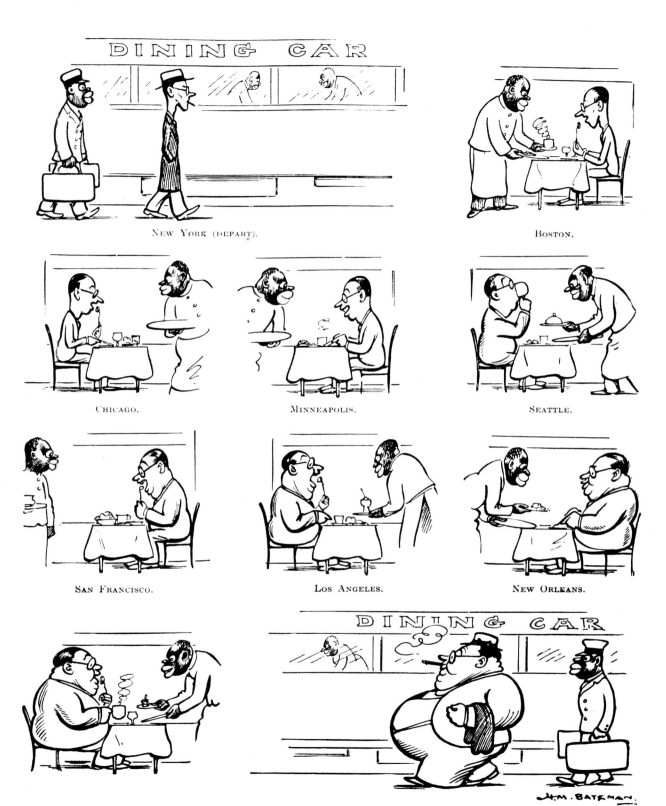

'THE ROUND TRIP – A SLIGHT TRIBUTE TO THE DINING CAR
SERVICE OF THE USA',
Punch, 9 May 1932.

'The Possibilities of a Vacuum Cleaner,' 'Getting a Document Stamped in Somerset House,' or 'The One Note Man,' which took up four or more pages and consisted of sixty separate frames. They are as near as one can get to the animated cartoon without actual animation. Interestingly, Walt Disney professed himself a great admirer of Bateman's work, and let him look around the studio and watch the animators – only sixteen of them at that time – as they worked on their drawings.

Bateman and his wife made all their long journeys in the States by train, and far from tiring of the constant travelling they found it as enjoyable as any other part of the trip. Bateman liked the 'luxurious Pullmans and the observation cars ... the meals served in the restaurant car and the negroes who waited on us so stylishly ...' On the Chief, a train of the Santa Fe railroad, he was given a drawing-room to himself, and a bed-sitting-room, and there were 'cars for lounging, cars for reading and writing, for work or play or observation ... a veritable first class hotel on wheels, confined some may think – I prefer to call it compact.'[6]

His train journeys inspired a number of cartoons which appeared in England on his return, among them 'The Couple who passed Reno without getting a Divorce,' 'The Round Trip,' and 'Seeing America.'

What precise influence, if any, America had on Bateman, or he on America, is difficult to assess. Certainly he acquired a taste for good ice-cream, and a great liking for the country and the people. John Jensen, in his collection of Bateman's work, wrote that Bateman had a considerable influence on the humorous style of the *New Yorker* in the early years from its first appearance in 1925. Gluyas Williams, for instance, used the 'Man Who ...' idea, and though his style was more muted and believable than Bateman's, without the latter's distortion, he had clearly looked carefully at Bateman's work.[7] Perhaps this had a little to do with Bateman's enthusiasm for the magazine. Assessing the state of American comic art, he wrote:

> At the time of my first visit in 1923 the humour struck me as being simple, rudimentary and lacking in subtlety, whilst the drawings were, with a few exceptions, rather crude.
>
> Soon after this came a big upward movement, which seemed to be established with the arrival of the *New Yorker*, a paper which I think has had more influence upon the trend of humour as it is produced in comic papers than any other in recent years. To my mind the *New Yorker* during the first year or two of its production was the livest publication of its kind throughout the world and marked the beginning of a new era.

This 'new era' of which he wrote, however, was losing its attraction for Bateman, and though throughout the 1930s there were many intimations that he was capable of highly inventive work, it became increasingly apparent after 1932 that he was losing his own interest in the art. By 1937, when he wrote his autobiography, *H. M. Bateman by Himself*, he felt that he had done what he had set out to do from that moment, at the age of thirteen, when he decided to 'make people laugh,' and during the 1930s and beyond he was to devote himself more and more to that still active dream of becoming a 'serious' artist.

15
THE ELUSIVE DREAM

After he returned from America, Bateman decided that he would devote his time in earnest to painting. Though his last cartoon for *Punch* appeared in 1934[1] and his last for *The Tatler* in 1936, and though he did continue to produce occasional work for many years, 1933 seems to have been the year of decision. It was in fact quite a full year for him, in which, among other things, he edited a book on Caran d'Ache, and wrote an Introduction to it (see chapter 10), and painted his extraordinary watercolour, 'The Mad Musician,' which was shown at the Royal Academy that year. He was also working on a set of illustrations for a book on fishing, *Fly-fishing for Duffers* by R. D. Peck.[2] However, though Bateman later claimed that it had been the horror of the Second World War that made him cease work as a humorous artist, he had really changed course long before that.

Not the least remarkable fact about such an early retirement – in 1933, he was forty-six – is that he managed to support his family, in no great luxury, it is true, and live the rest of his long life almost entirely on the proceeds of his work as a cartoonist. Over the next thirty years, he lived off royalties and interest: he earned comparatively little, though he did continue to work for advertisers and old friends for some time.[3] That he was no longer earning a great deal added another dimension to his already 'careful' disposition. His paintings were by no means as financially rewarding as his cartoons, nor did he mean them to be. His desire was not to make his fortune but, in all humility, to create something beautiful and delicate in a medium he had always loved. As a young man he had made the difficult decision to become a humorous, rather than a serious, artist – a decision that caused him much pain – but he had never managed to subdue his early inclinations. By 1933 he felt that it was a case of 'now or never'. He wanted to paint a picture in the manner of Sisley, or Lucien Pissarro, whom he had met and admired. At the end of his autobiography he wrote:

And yet I confess, like most people, I am not entirely satisfied. There is still something missing in which I could wish for fulfilment – and I will tell you what it is.

I would like to have painted a quite serious picture; one that did not depend upon any sort of comic situation to make it appeal.

I don't mean a subject picture that would make you cry, for, unlike the majority of comedians, I have no desire at all to try to play Hamlet.

The picture I have in mind is quite a simple one. A landscape perhaps, with just the way light falls on a house or a tree, almost anything would do for a subject so long as it expresses the beauty of earth and sky and water, so that it would charm you.

'THE MAD MUSICIAN.'

In September 1933, he set off in pursuit of this romantic vision. He packed a small bag, took his fishing rod, a folding stool and his materials, and made his way by train towards the Pyrenees, and into the wilder regions of Spain. The letters he wrote to his wife on this and subsequent trips in 1934 and 1935 – he stayed each time for about three months – reveal him as solitary, penny-pinching, selfishly caught up in his dream, but above all grappling with something he really knew would always elude him.

[October 1933. From a hotel in the Pyrenees.]

A perfect gem of a place and subjects to paint everywhere. But I am not sure I shall stay on for more than a day or two as the place is rather too popular for my liking. The hotel is quite full with holiday people and the town itself is stiff with artists and if there is one thing above all others I want to avoid just for a little bit it's fellows sufferers!

[October 1933. Hotel Marina, Spain.]

I'm more or less getting used now to working with a huge crowd around me – the curiosity of the Spaniards is amazing – it is absolutely insatiable. One appears to be almost alone on setting out, but the instant one stops and starts to set up the easel people have sprung up from everywhere – every tiniest movement is noted with goggling eyes and remarked upon! ... I expect to go down to Alicante by way of Valencia.

[November 1935. Puerto de Santa Maria, Cadiz, Spain.]

At first the evenings were rather long here, but I have got a small boy to come in and sit for me for about an hour each day and give him 30 centimos (about 2d) which he is quite satisfied with!

[December 1, 1935. As above.]

The past week has been a good one ... I have managed to carry a couple of things out. ... I was not too well though at the beginning of the week and had to spend Thursday in bed. It was a touch of the old stomach trouble and just for a bit made me feel very anxious. ... The last week has really been a good one and I shall be able to pack up feeling reasonably satisfied. But you mustn't expect to see a bundle of masterpieces unrolled before your eyes – I don't think I do as well now as last time out here – but I'll let you judge.

[December 7, 1935. Paris.]

Went to the Luxembourg this morning and to the Autumn Salon this afternoon, which is the biggest and most awful show I've ever seen – I only wish you could have seen some of the pictures, as I know you would have screamed with laughter at them – they were frightful! But judging by the number, it seems as if half the population of France is composed of painters.

[Monday, December 9, 1935. Paris.]

... as for your suggestion about my staying on over Christmas, far from taking it in the wrong way I am really touched, very much, for your loving and generous thought for me. (Incidentally it just makes me want to be with you all the more.) As it happens I was already thinking very strongly of staying on for a bit longer than at first seemed likely, as I find so much here to interest me and since writing to you on Saturday have been to see several artists, who are all ready to give some lessons. ...

Who do you think I met today in a studio? Someone far more important and interesting than the Prince of Wales, or Mussolini: Cezanne's son!! I almost fainted, and as for you – well, you would have shrieked with laughter at the funny old fat thing. This really is a wonderful place for artists. Went to lunch today with Routier – he is a nice fellow and quite a recluse, but says he will come to see us for a day or two. ...

Anyway I fancy you'll have me wishing everybody a Merry Christmas or Xmas, or whatever the damn thing is, with a fixed grin. Again thanks, Darling, for your sweet letter and with all love and blessings.

Your same old Mayo ...

[Wednesday, December 18, 1935. Paris.]

My Dearest Bren

I don't expect to be hanging out my stocking in bracing Berks next Tuesday, so am now sending a cheque for Christmas presents and shall be glad if you would hand them out for me.

Nanny	*1. 0.0*
Jesse	*10.0*
Deacon	*7.6*
Postman	*7.6*
Diana	*5.–*
Monica	*5.–*
Father	*5.– (or ¼ lb of tobacco)*
Mum	*3.6*
Brida	*3.6*
Tom Iremonger	*2.– (two oz of tobacco)*

3. 9.6 [sic]

... I work each day from the model, under a fierce sort of teacher, but the Lord knows what progress I make – only a mess I think! and return in the evening in various moods of elation, depression or mystification. ...

[Friday, December 19, 1935. Paris.]

... what one really needs is two years here, and a month or two is hardly a nibble. But I'll see. ...

I think you are a bit wrong about my attitude towards Christmas, which seems to suggest I am rather a Scrooge – I like a good deal of Christmas really, but not too much of it, and I must say that nowadays children are often spoiled over it. ...

I feel anxious about you often and hate being away from you for so long, but it's now or never with me for Art and I steel myself to stay away till the dregs of the cup are drained! (As a matter of fact I shall never even sip the blooming cup, as you would soon realize if you saw the shows of work here, but I like to kid myself and I may achieve those quiet little watercolours you once predicted for my old age.)

Well, avanti! Avanti! whatever it means and all love.[4]

Though he realized his paintings were by no means the perfect things he desired them to be, Bateman was confident enough to put them together for an exhibition in London, in 1936, at the Leicester Galleries. His reputation as a cartoonist was enough to ensure that they were shown, and, of course, 1936 was the year of the Spanish Civil War, which no doubt added to their interest. He exhibited seventy of his paintings: both oils and watercolours.

Bateman returned to England not only with a bundle of paintings but also with some form of lingering food poisoning. As always when his health was bad, he sank into a deep depression, helped on by a general lack of enthusiasm over his exhibition, and became intolerant and intolerable at home, wrapping himself in black dejection. The repressed anxiety of which he was always a victim was now often expressed in violent rage against his wife and petty tyranny over his children, to whom he sometimes seemed a stranger. This abuse of his family may very possibly have been the misplaced expression of his deep feelings for them, but that was no consolation at the time: his wife's health became affected, and his children walked in fear of incurring his temper. Even when well, he could be remarkably insensitive to their feelings and needs. His wife had no money of her own, and had continually to fight to get the necessary funds from him: he used her financial dependence like a weapon against her. He was not, however, without tenderness: he had a pet dormouse, and a little dog, and he could also be delightful and kind towards his family – but he grew terribly moody, and jealous of their laughter. It became a relief when he went away, the dreadful possessiveness and the general moratorium on all fun and games were suddenly gone.

In 1934, the family had moved from Reigate to Curridge, near Newbury, in Berkshire: they had been looking for some time for somewhere more peaceful and rural. Here Bateman had a large old coach house as a studio, and used to erect peculiar structures in the garden so that he could paint outside even when it rained. He went for long walks almost every day, took his sketch-book, and drew the local farms, the animals, and the old barns, full of sacks and machinery.

He also settled down to write his autobiography, which appeared in 1937. It is not a long book, and in many ways not very revealing, but signified a public acknowledgement that his career as a cartoonist was really over. It was serialized in the *News Chronicle* on publication.

His last large gesture as H. M. Bateman, celebrated and popular cartoonist, took place toward the end of 1938, when he decided with his agent to organize an exhibition of his work in Sydney, Australia. To get there he went by boat and train across Europe, North Africa, India and Asia, and came back by way of New Zealand, Canada and America. He was away from home for nine months, returning just before the outbreak of war.

His outward journey passed without much incident: his letters home were almost bored. He caught a fever in Singapore, which laid him low for some time, but once in Australia he received a most pleasant surprise. He had, of course, been born there, and every newspaper in the country made much of him as the famous Australian artist returning home – though he had left when eighteen months old – a reaction he did little to discourage. He was constantly reviewed and interviewed, gave radio broadcasts and public lectures, and went to endless official receptions. At one of these, in Sydney, groups of schoolgirls, dressed in red uniforms, re-enacted 'The Guardsman Who dropped It.' It was all most pleasing, and during the two months that he stayed – March and April 1939 – he hardly had a moment's peace. In March, he wrote home to his wife:

> I am having the greatest possible success, and from the moment I touched Australia at Fremantle, I have literally had a triumphal progress across the Continent! In Perth, Adelaide and Melbourne I

Paintings by Bateman.

Left and Below Left:
Spanish interior and street
scene painted during his
visit to Spain, 1935.

Opposite:
The interior of an old barn,
painted probably during the
late 1930s.

was interviewed and photographed continually. . . . Telegrams have showered on me and my first day in Sydney yesterday was one long 'racking' by the press. There are more articles in the papers about me than I know of!! It is really comic and I find it amusing and gratifying as it's the first time I've been made a fuss of and it will be some time before I begin to get tired of it. You can think of me out here in a huge whirl of enthusiasm.[5]

Later, during April 1939, when his exhibition opened, the fuss was still going on. He wrote more letters home, delighted with his success, angry that people were being too slow in actually buying his cartoons, full of remarks about what they should or should not be doing at home while he was away, and anxious for himself at the threat of war.

I seem to be writing to you in another strained period in Europe – Hitler having done the dirty and I only hope that I shall be home before it actually breaks out. Personally, I'm still an optimist, but Germany has shown itself so unreliable in its word that there is no knowing what the lust for power may lead them to do in the future. . . . Big crowds of people have visited my show. . . . I have made a little in other ways here. The people are appreciative and I'm a big 'noise'. . . . You must see that your letters are not overweight – I had to pay on the last one.[6]

He returned home in the summer, stopping at New Zealand, Samoa, Honolulu, Canada, where he travelled by train from Vancouver to Montreal, and lastly the United States. He took the boat from New York, and arrived back in England not long before war was declared, in September 1939.

One of the first things he did was sit down and write a book about his travels, called simply *World Tour*,[7] which was never published. It is a very ordinary travel book, not without certain flashes of insight and some interesting information, but it hardly does him justice, and even the sketches of his trip were rather perfunctory. He seems to have travelled in rather a daze, which is understandable, since he hardly had time to adjust to one new impression before another thrust itself upon him.

Soon after this, in 1940, he wrote a similar book on England, called *On the Move in England*, which was published, but suffered from the same over-speedy blurring of vision.[8] It contained many good passages, however, and was serialized in the *Sunday Times*. It was a genial and amusing book, but there were far more interesting and important things happening all around him, for the War had now descended in earnest, and the book was written in rather a dash, as though something to be done and got over quickly.

Perhaps another reason for the book's lack of conviction was the death of his father in that year, an event which shook Bateman to the core, and left him weeping and miserable for many months, oppressed partly with a sense of his own guilt at having been neglectful of him for so long. The relationship between son and father had been tense and full of unspoken complication for many years, especially on the side of the son. Brenda always had to battle, against passionate opposition, to invite father

Bateman for Christmas or for other such occasions. Strangely, as soon as the old man arrived, he and his son got on extremely well, and were obviously very fond of one another – though Bateman was always jealous of his father's slightest show of paternalism towards Brenda or the family. He would not allow him to give them presents, saying that if there was anything they needed he would provide. Of course, it was not a question of need but of kindliness, which seemed to escape him.

Whatever the underlying reason – perhaps a still continuing loyalty to his mother, who would have nothing to do with her husband, and never saw him – Bateman behaved badly towards his father, and, though he loved him, kept him at arm's length. Death provoked a whole complex of feeling, of grief and remorse, which overwhelmed Bateman, and left him weak and uncertain.

The War itself he referred to only as 'this Ghastly Business,' it merely adding to his irritability and melancholy. He became an A.R.P. warden, which he hated. He also hated the many evacuees coming from the towns and spilling over his beloved countryside.

The world was upside down, and he tried to bury himself in his painting. But it was not going well, and in 1943 he decided he needed to go back to school. There was then a peculiar period when he enrolled at the Ruskin College of Fine Art and Drawing, in Oxford, and tried to re-establish his roots in academic method. While he was there, he met the artist Stanley Parker, who wrote a long article about him for the *Oxford Mail*. He saw Bateman at an exhibition of Contemporary French Art at the Ashmolean, and asked the Master of Drawing at the Ruskin, Albert Rutherston, what Bateman was doing.

> 'You'd better ask him,' smiled Albert Rutherston and introduced us.
>
> 'I'm learning to paint,' said the most famous humorous artist of the day. And sure enough there he was squeezing his tubes on to his palette, wiping his hands on his smock, fixing his easel, no more of a star than the fifty other pupils round him. ... The war for him is obviously a period of gestation. When it is over, and his new ideas are let loose, we shall see, I predict, a bigger and better Bateman than before.[9]

As far as Bateman's artistic efforts were concerned, Stanley Parker was unfortunately wrong – though Bateman never ceased trying.

The people who suffered most while Bateman was struggling with himself were his family. He was unhappy and depressed, and became rather a terrifying figure. His younger daughter, Monica, remembers this as a most difficult time.

> As a child I was certainly afraid of him, as he was unpredictably moody, sometimes roaring uncontrollably with laughter at some simple jokes I did not always understand, but more often he was withdrawn and morose, disapproving of everything, complaining about the cost of things, the bad weather, the noise we made, the clothes we wore, our friends; he seemed to me to be most often rather unhappy.[10]

DIANA.
A portrait of the artist's
elder daughter.

Bateman was not a family man. He felt hemmed in by the three women, who seemed to form a united body against him, and was confused by emotions he never really tried to understand. He became at the same time reclusive yet possessive: refusing to go out, or making a scene when he did, yet, on the other hand, not allowing his wife to invite friends home, most of whom he disliked or at least pretended to dislike – expecially the women, though always jealous of any small attentions his wife might receive from the men. He permitted her one dinner party a year, at Christmas, and made that as difficult as possible.

Once, on a freezing night, he removed all the coals from the fire just before his guests arrived, saying that he would not waste money on such people, and made them all sit shivering through the evening. He had gone a little mad. He seemed especially to be affected by the full moon: during the week or so leading up to it he was at his most unpredictable.

In 1946, after one terrible scene, in which he wrecked his elder daughter's eighteenth birthday celebrations because he said she had used too many matches to light the candles on her cake, his wife, Brenda, finally realized that they had to part. She had just been left an inheritance by Harry Collison, whom she had nursed through a final illness, and was now in a position to stand up for herself. Bateman had used his purse-strings to bind his family tightly to him, but lost them anyway, not really knowing what to do with them when he had them so closely under his control.

It was not only his family: even his painting was affected – he could not bring himself to spend sufficient money on his oil colours, so that his pictures often looked rather thin.

His mania made him not only miserly but paranoid, and he associated his sense of persecution more and more completely, as the years went by, with one particular body, until he saw in it almost all the evils from which his world suffered: the Department of Inland Revenue.

16
THE TAX MAN

Bateman's relationship with the Inland Revenue, a relationship which became more tortuous as he grew older, dates from the very early days of his career. As a young man just beginning to receive an appreciable income from his work, he took himself off, conscientiously, to his local Office of Taxation to declare that he had now become a proper subject for its attention. He was dealt with by a condescending official, who asked if he had come for a 'good whipping,' and sent him brusquely on his way. This was not a good tactic to adopt with Bateman, who liked public servants to remember they were servants, and who was generally, except to those nearest to him, a most courteous man. He was also not the sort of person to forget or forgive such an incident. He resolved never again to do anything that might be construed as even remotely helpful to the Revenue authorities – and, moreover, to get the better of them as much as possible.

The first in the series of contests which arose between Bateman and the Inland Revenue Department took place during the Great War, probably in late 1915 or early 1916. The details are not now clear (see chapter 9), but Bateman appears to have come through unscathed, though not without some misgivings, which he turned to good profit in his cartoon 'The False Income Tax Return.'

The next few income tax returns went by undisputed, and Bateman made little reference to the Department or its minions in his work. But then, in 1921, probably because he now felt more sure of himself, more secure, and had started to earn large sums from his work and so had more to be taken from him, he took a very large risk indeed – the consequence of which was that he narrowly escaped imprisonment and had to pay a really heavy fine: some £4,000. The penalty would have been much greater had not the Department's officials, in their overexcitement, greatly exaggerated the true amount wanting. Nevertheless, it was a nasty blow to purse and pride.

It should be understood that Bateman, though never happy to part with his money, was a scrupulously honest man except in this one respect, and that he had come to regard income tax as State-controlled theft which he had every right to resist, and against which he had almost a moral obligation to take up arms. 1921, then, saw the real beginning of his battle against the State and the Inland Revenue – a battle which he waged with the pen, both in drawing and writing, continuously until his death in 1970.

The 1921 affair had many repercussions, and dragged on until well after Bateman was married, in 1926. His bitterness would sometimes reach manic levels. He begged his wife to promise that in the event of his death through suicide, which he occasionally contemplated, or from other causes

'THE WARD',
1923.

no doubt equally unhappy, she should alert the public in unequivocal
terms to the truth: that he had been unmercifully, gleefully, hounded to
his death by the Inland Revenue – that after years of villainous persecution
the strain had finally proved too great.

That same quality of mind which begat such wholehearted enthusiasm
in his youth led him in middle-age dangerously towards melancholic
obsession. The tax man as a figure of depraved and malicious cruelty
began to haunt him, and he turned out a steady stream of venomous
cartoons on the long-nosed, sharp-toothed, bestial tax official. Some of
these drawings were so overpoweringly hateful that even Bateman, and
certainly his wife, realized they were rather too revealing – that he had
overburdened the subject with spleen – and so he took them out and

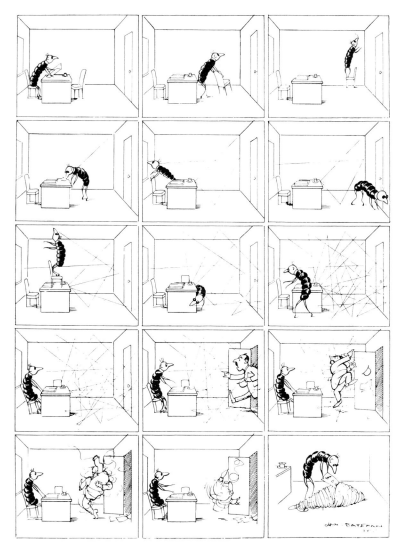

'THE INCOME TAX WORM
AT WORK',
1925.

burned them. Also, somewhat strangely since he was now mostly involved
in the more delicate pursuit of landscape painting, his tax officials, as
though to emphasize their nastiness, were often crudely drawn and luridly
coloured – so perhaps art and taste combined to put some to the fire.

By the 1940s, writing about his preoccupations came almost as
naturally to Bateman as introducing them into his cartoons, and over the
succeeding years he produced essays and stories which, while they might
fall slightly short of the standard set by the heaviest of his drawings, leave
one in no doubt of his opinions.

One story, unpublished, called 'The Other Man,' was written in
1953,[1] at his little cottage in Sampford Courtenay (see next chapter). Here
he lived a very isolated life, and spent a great deal of his time in solitary

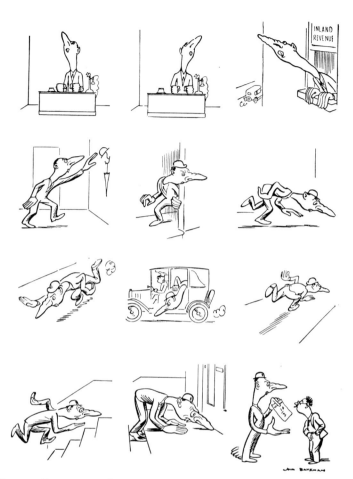

'STUDIES OF AN INCOME TAX
INSPECTOR TRACKING
A HALFPENNY',
Punch, 20 September 1933.

walks over Dartmoor, where he must have felt very much like the Earth's sole inhabitant. The story is about the only survivor of an unspecified but comprehensive catastrophe who tries to re-establish some sort of normal existence. He collects canned food from the ruins, builds himself a makeshift home, and somehow starts a small farm, with a few goats and chickens. He goes for long walks, but never sees another person, and eventually settles down to cultivate his crops. Each morning, however, he scans the surrounding countryside with a telescope in the hope that one day he might spot another human being. He has been living like this for a considerable time, when at last, one morning, through his telescope, he sees another man:

> My heart leaped in my breast and tears of emotion were coursing down my cheeks as I rushed forward to meet him. . . . He was now plainly visible jumping over the debris of a past civilization – already I could hear him trying to make me understand something. What was it? I recognized the sound of words but their meaning was still beyond me. I struggled to recover the faculty of verbal intercourse.

Now he was quite close to me and I saw that he waved a paper – a paper of ugly colour in one hand. Suddenly I felt a queer sensation of nervousness and stepped backwards to the entrance of the house. He came quickly up the last few yards of the slope and as his approaching voice grew louder the gates of my memory were unlocked and I realized what it was he was saying to me:

'I am H.M. Inspector of Taxes. You do not appear to have rendered a return of income for the past twelve months. I shall require it within ten days.'

But Bateman did not always deal so metaphorically with taxation and its officers. Images of tax men as birds of prey, as stoats, as sniffing, tracking, dog-like, rat-like creatures were very satisfying on an imaginative level, but left something to be desired on a rational one. Sensing this, he tried occasionally to argue the matter in more reasonable terms. It was always, of course, a highly emotive subject, and he suffered from a feeling of almost deadly oppression.

In another unpublished essay, probably from the early 1960s, he
wrote:

> From time immemorial taxation has been hated, feared and evaded as
> far as possible. In histories of the past there are constant references to
> people groaning under the burdens of taxation, of revolts when the
> load they staggered under was too great for them to support, and of
> joy, relief and thanksgiving when some portion of the load at least was
> removed just sufficiently to ease the strain. But how rarely that
> reduction happened; instead it has been a tale of increase and new
> methods of extortion in every way.
>
> Of all forms that taxation takes Income Tax is by far the most
> penal. When Income Tax was introduced the politician who invented
> it said to himself that as time went on no tax would cause so much
> misery, dissent and trouble as this would. How right he was. At the
> time of its inception it stood at one penny in the pound and only a
> limited section of the country's population was called upon to pay it.
> Income Tax has come on wonderfully since then – not a soul who can
> rub two sous together escapes it.
>
> Income Tax is like a malignant growth, a cancer, to which man is
> heir and subject when he is born into this world; but whereas not every
> man or woman becomes a victim of the physical, bodily scourger, if he
> does suffer he can in many cases be saved from the worst consequences
> of it, not one of us escapes the attention and onslaught of the Taxman.
>
> Something has surely gone wrong with our concept of civilization
> when two parties cannot get together for a transaction without a third
> unseen party being present, a party who does nothing in creating the
> business or furthering it but who will have to be reckoned with
> eventually. In everyday life a modicum of courtesy, consideration and
> good manners is appreciated and needed to prevent friction. But the
> manners and method of the Income Tax are quite extraordinary – they
> are such that would not be tolerated for a moment in all other walks of
> life. Income Tax authorities speak a peculiar language of their own, a
> kind of language within a language; even the orders they issue are
> unintelligible to the average taxpayer, who has to employ an expert to
> unravel the complexities of the demands made upon him and to steer
> him clear of the traps set for him. And woe betide him if in his
> ignorance or through laxity or in any spirit of levity, quite apart from
> any intent to deceive, he should blunder into one of the traps within
> the maze along which he is compelled to wander.
>
> If a man works he should be rewarded not punished; yet the harder
> he works the more he is punished – a Gilbertian situation if ever there
> was one ... it seems idiotic that once a year we have to sit down and
> render an account to someone unseen of what we have spent and how
> much we have received. 'Please, Sir, I made fourpence halfpenny here.
> Yes, Sir, I spent threepence there. No, Sir, there's nothing more, so
> help me, God, Sir.' Oh to be in England now that April the 5th is
> here.[2]

In fact Bateman was not in England any more – he had gone to live in Gozo (see next chapter) – but ironically, in those last years of his life, instead of escaping from his worries, they pursued him over the seas. At one moment there seemed a danger of his beneficiaries having to pay double death duties – once to the British Government and once to the Maltese – and a good deal of the surviving correspondence from those years consists of replies from bank managers and accountants to Bateman's requests for help and advice. His complaint, his sense of persecution, was not without foundation. The final irony was that probably the last letter he received before his death in February 1970 was a Notice of Assessment from the Maltese Commissioner of Inland Revenue.

Taxation, then, came to represent the whole oppressive structure of a system of government which interfered with and controlled the life of the citizen; and so the deformed creatures that had started as tax officials came also to take on the roles of bureaucrat, planner and administrator. Bateman remained ever a reactionary Edwardian, and the same issues that had been of such concern when Lloyd George and his fellows first introduced the Welfare State, remained just as stark and vital in the 1950s and 1960s: above all, should the State interfere with the life of the individual? After the end of the Second World War, and the coming to power of a Labour Government, for Bateman this question became and continued to be a major preoccupation. The sometime gentle social commentator had become committed to a vehement political attitude.

It was in 1945 that Bateman first became associated with a group called the Society of Individualists and National League for Freedom, which published numerous pamphlets and leaflets, and eventually a magazine called *Freedom First*. This hardline, right-wing publication was the perfect vehicle for Bateman's anti-State cartoons. His feelings on the oppressiveness of the Modern State had shown themselves in his work over a number of years. He had a dark Kafka-like horror of the State official and State offices, and his favourite metaphor for modern society became the image of the maze. When his strong feelings were tempered by an ironic humour, he could produce a comic materpiece like 'Getting a document stamped at Somerset House.'

'In the Maze.'

'THE BOY –
WHAT WILL HE BECOME?
(AND THE GIRL, TOO?)
THE STATE EQUALISER.'

Opposite and following pages:
'GETTING A DOCUMENT STAMPED
AT SOMERSET HOUSE' – I–IV,
The Tatler, 30 November 1923.

Though he despised the romantic attempts at non-conformity among the youth of the 1960s, Bateman thought that individuality and beauty were being rigorously expunged by an army of Government officials who sought to make everyone and everything conform to a standard pattern. He was especially dismayed by the effects of 'progress' on the English countryside, the old buildings and old villages of England. He compared the Government in its treatment of these to a painting by Goya, in the Prado, of Satan devouring his own children. 'It might occur to anyone to wonder,' he wrote, 'why Satan is doing this terrible thing, which, even for Satan seems unnatural. But Goya's expressiveness has left no shadow of doubt as to the reason. Satan is mad.'[3]

Bateman by no means rejected all progress: he thought scientific advance exciting, and, for example, considered the first Moon landing the most wonderful feat of his lifetime – he never stopped talking about it. It was the ugly, levelling, concrete and tarmac side of progress that he hated, and it upset him so much that it was without doubt one of the major factors in his decision to quit England, eventually for good. The countryside he had spent so many hours and days walking through, fishing in and sketching, the people and customs he had so wonderfully described and made fun of were all changing, and he felt no more entirely at home.

A NEW START

After Bateman left his family in 1947 he went to Langport, in Somerset, where relatives of his mother lived, rented a small house, and almost immediately fell ill with prostate trouble. He had an operation, spent some weeks in hospital, and then went to convalesce at his mother's in Reigate. Though now very elderly, and troubled with rheumatism, she was still a powerful personality, remembered by her grandchildren as someone to be avoided at all costs.

The years that followed were like a slow recovery from a long illness, for, apart from his continuing obsession with the Inland Revenue and related matters, Bateman became far more peaceful, reconciled to himself and to his lot. After convalescence, he moved back to Curridge until the house was sold, in 1951; Brenda and Monica had gone to live in London, and Diana had married and was living in Bath. Then he moved on to a house in Shabbington, not far from Oxford, until at last, in 1953, he found a real home for himself, in a tiny thatched cottage: Brook Cottage, in the little village of Sampford Courtenay, on the edge of Dartmoor.

He acquired a housekeeper to look after him, a Mrs Maynard, who was 'really good, quiet, contented and considerate.' It was just what he needed: peace, independence and little responsibility. For almost the first time he was able to relate to his daughters and they to him. No longer in such close proximity, matters previously dark became clearer and understood. Both girls had gone to art college, and he became terribly proud of their work, saying, 'I wish I could draw like that,' with a real humility, as though all of his achievement had somehow never been. He was starting again.

With Monica, his younger daughter, he went on painting holidays to St Ives, in Cornwall, and one winter to Southern Italy for the warmth; it snowed all the time and they painted wrapped in layers of overcoats and scarves, festooned with hot water bottles. She enjoyed travelling with him, found him most companionable, though shy of other people, whom he still observed with the critical eye of the caricaturist.

Bateman even started a little commissioned work again. He did some illustrations for another book on fishing,[1] without much enthusiasm, though glad of the money. His life was on the whole quiet and contemplative now. In all weathers he would walk over the moor for many miles with his little dog, Tim. When it was fine he might paint outside; he invented a special contraption which hung from his neck, rather like a pedlar's tray, on which he could rest his paper and paint while standing, and so did not have to bother putting up an easel.

Much of his time was given up to writing. He produced essays on painting, on keeping notes, on success, on inspiration, on change and travel for the artist, on income tax, of course, on the importance of practice, on the decline in narrative painting and in standards of portraiture, on the pretentiousness of analysis, and on many other topics. He also wrote *Homes from Home* (see chapter 14) an anecdotal book on his many hours in hotels. Having spent so much time travelling, he was something of an expert. He liked hotels, they suited his temperament: ideal places in which to watch the world go by, without having to become involved. They also provided a curious no-man's-land or place of freedom for the emotions.

He relates a story about 'a friend' (almost certainly himself) who broke down and cried in a hotel bedroom after a long period of strain.

> . . . as he sat alone in the room, with a suitcase and a few other of his belongings around him, thoughts of his past troubles and the uncertainty of the future crowded in on him and overwhelmed him. Outside in the street was the constant hum of passing traffic. Inside, all around within a few yards of him, muted sounds made him aware of never-ending activities – a door was opened, voices could be heard, footsteps along the corridor, a bell ringing somewhere. Suddenly it seemed the whole complexity of human existence became apparent. The unreasoning insistence of these banal items would intrude and govern him until the end of it all. He gave way under the thought of it and wept . . . the lapse did him good.

Like his essays, the book was never published, nor does it seem that he ever tried to get it into print. In 1956, however, when he was sixty-nine, he started to write his best book, *The Evening Rise*, which was published by Duckworth in 1960. Subtitled 'Fifty Years of Fly-Fishing,' the book is full of amusing incidents more or less connected with his fishing days, instructive, and held together by consistent enthusiasm on all matters pertaining to fly-fishing. He refers to it as his 'passionate pursuit,' and indeed his love of everything to do with the sport, the eccentric fellow fishermen he knew, the rivers and countryside where he found his favourite spots, the skill and concentration demanded, the machinery of rods and reels and flies, all combine to re-create a private world full of enjoyment which still continued to offer him many pleasurable experiences in his seventieth year.

In that same year, his mother died, at the age of ninety-two. He took her death very calmly, attended to everything himself, and only informed his children of the event some time after the funeral had taken place. Whether because of her great age, or his own advancing years, or because he had less with which to reproach himself, he seemed to cope far better with his mother's than with his father's death.

While at Brook Cottage, though living a simple and retiring life, he soon became known among a section of the local community, and formed a close though not familiar friendship with a retired colonel, Colonel Stable, with whom he would often go fishing on the East or West Okement, up on the moor. Colonel Stable was as unlike one of Bateman's old colonels as could possibly be – quiet and courteous, a keen naturalist, who spent much of his time looking at birds and butterflies – and their relationship was

'FISHING',
1916.

based on an unspoken respect for each other's privacy. Colonel Stable
remembers Bateman as a man of quiet moods and limited sociability, but
of an essentially cheerful disposition, who took great pleasure in many
things: in his fishing and sketching, of course, in smoking his pipe, and in
talking.

One of the topics that came under consideration was the possibility of
leaving England, not only because of the increasing despoliation of the
countryside, the income tax, and the rampant socialism of the inhabitants,
but also because of the winter weather. Bateman now suffered from
occasional bouts of asthmatic bronchitis, and he was anxious about the
cold and damp within and without his little cottage.

In 1957, he decided on a long trip abroad, and left in July for France,

'A Vital Mistake.' The figure in this cartoon is William Caine.

with the idea of moving farther south as the autumn approached. He stayed at a small friendly inn in the country of the Lot, where he painted for three months, but on going through Provence towards Italy, in September, he found that he could no longer cope with the travelling. Very despondent, he turned back for England just at the wrong season. He later wrote from Sampford Courtenay to his younger daughter, Monica, who had married and emigrated to Canada, that it was 'all very sudden and disappointing. ... The whole of the South of France is developed for tourism and in my view is completely ruined for the artist, and the volume of motor traffic and the noise everywhere is appalling. ... The fact is, my dear, that I realize I am now too old for knocking about abroad alone and am better off in my own burrow in spite of its drawbacks. It's a regular defeat.'[2]

By January of the next year, however, he was already thinking of taking his car abroad, to motor through France and Italy, in order to find a place to settle down, but though he made many plans, and did manage to go on expeditions to Cornwall, and Suffolk, and to the South coast, he did not actually manage to leave England again until 1964. Part of the reason for this was the bother, part that he was not always in the best of health to move around very much, but also that he was busy.

He found himself in the rather peculiar situation of watching a revival of interest in his old cartoons within his own lifetime, and he was brushing the dust off them and sorting them out as people appeared at his cottage eager to buy his originals. The Arts Council mounted a touring exhibition of cartoonists, in which he was well represented, and the Fine Art Society, in London, asked him for an exhibition, which ran from December 1962 to January 1963, and was a huge success. Two thirds of the cartoons in this were sold on the first day, and by the end practically everything on the walls had gone – over seventy drawings – and even work they had no space to hang, that had been kept behind unframed, had mostly been bought. The gallery kept asking Bateman for more. 'It really is pleasing,' he wrote to his daughter, Monica, 'and rather surprising as I've been out of the limelight for some time now. ... My show has proved an astonishing success.'[3] The following year he was presented with the Cartoonists' Club Award.

Despite all this recognition, which delighted him, he was not becoming any happier in England. He thought it overcrowded and common, and after a brief escape to Brittany his appetite for change was whetted once more, and he decided to try somewhere completely unknown, with the promise of sunshine and quiet. He had been preparing for this move for some time, had sold his little cottage and moved into rooms in a nearby farm. Now a friend suggested Malta to him and, seized by the spirit of adventure, he packed his painting gear and a few clothes, and in some excitement set off by train towards his new home. He liked Malta immediately. Though it was autumn when he arrived, the weather was perfect, the bright colours and intense light challenged him, and he struggled to put them on to canvas. It was a wonderful escape from the 'rain, the overcrowding and the politics.'

He soon moved across to Gozo, the neighbouring, smaller island, much less populous, and with a more interesting and varied landscape.

There was a distinctly British feeling about the island, with many expatriates, and square red telephone boxes. Edward Lear, who had been painting on both the islands more than a hundred years earlier (1865), thought Malta had 'practically no scenery' but found that Gozo had coast scenery which 'may truly be called pomskizillious and gromphibberous, being as no words can describe its magnificence.'[4] In such happy surroundings, Bateman found himself at once at home: the kindliness and friendliness of the Gozithans, the perfect climate, the peace, made him calmer and happier than he had been for many years. He soon became a familiar and somewhat striking figure, tramping about in his heavy English shoes, and wearing what appeared to be the inner-lining of an old British Warm, topped with an ancient Spanish beret.

Though at first he moved between different hotels, he soon settled into the Royal Lady Hotel, at Mgarr, where, having dispossessed himself of most of his belongings in England, he lived very simply, but freely, in the room with the finest view. The hotel soon became decorated with his paintings, and in duller moments he would amaze the staff by executing impromptu tap-dances in the lounge.

Painting of Gozo.

He became much less unsociable here, much more approachable, and the British residents and many of the summer visitors to the island became extremely fond of him. He was like an old monarch holding court in exile, with all the pleasures of his office and none of its burdens – though in no way proud of his past glory. He gave paintings to visiting vicars for charity fêtes, and was pleased when these fetched thirty shillings. Colonel Stable, who had been persuaded to spend his winters on Gozo, remembered Bateman at Brook Cottage as hardly ever having visitors, but found him now far less lonely. Though Bateman returned to England briefly in the summers of 1966 and 1967, he did so not out of nostalgia but to escape the heat, tidy his affairs, and visit his grandchildren. He thought England got 'worse all the time.'

He was still very active, and most of his time was spent walking, drawing and painting – never anything grand: just village life, houses and donkeys. The actual paintings did not seem to matter so much to him now: certainly the idea of living up to some preconceived notion of success or

126. NEW COVERED PARADE, HASTINGS.

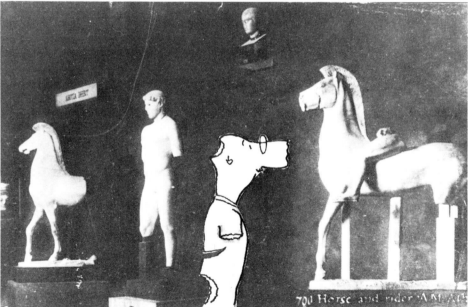

700 Horse and rider A.M.

POSTCARDS TO HIS GRANDCHILDREN

Above:
Horse and rider, Athens.
Bateman's message on the reverse reads: 'There – see what travel does for you! Knocks the corners off and makes
you a different person. Of course, the bottom may drop out of it some time.'

Top:
New Covered Parade, Hastings.

standard of achievement ceased to matter at all. He thought his work
'small stuff.' Yet he continued to paint and draw – it was his way of life, his
way of relating to the world around. He painted for the sake of painting, in
a meditative though still compulsive fashion. What mattered was not so
much what he did to the painting but what it did to him: the activity itself
became more important than the result.

Yet he still sought new impressions, new experiences. Having spent
some years of caution in England, feeling he was too old to go 'knocking
about,' in these last few years of his life he happily took himself off on
voyages much more arduous than he had then ever contemplated. He
went, during the summer of 1968, to visit his daughter, Monica, and her
family in Canada – by boat, for he would not fly – and found everything
there exhilarating, especially the space and the enormous trees. Then the
next summer he went alone to the Cycladic islands, staying on Paros and
Siros: the light was 'very strong, dazzling.' He was constantly at his easel,
sitting in some shaded place, trying to capture effects of the light that
seemed to mesmerize him.

He returned to his hotel on Gozo, in the autumn of 1969, having had a
most enjoyable time in Greece, keen and active in body and spirit. But he
had perhaps some intimation that his death was not far off, for he gave a
party for all his friends on the island, to thank them for their kindness to
him. In view of his still cautious economy, and his ungregarious nature,
this was a quite dramatic gesture. Not long after, in January 1970, he wrote
to Monica that he had not been quite well of late.

> ... had a bad cold before Christmas, with perhaps a bit of flu which I
> still have not properly recovered from; so had the doctor check me
> over last week – he thought my heart a bit low and promptly put me on
> to pills which I dislike taking but they are already doing me some
> good. [5]

He wrote also that he thought Malta was getting overcrowded, and that it
was only a matter of time before Gozo went the same way.

> It seems that there is nowhere left in the world where peace and
> simplicity can be found – it has all got to be standardized to a sort of
> luxury.

A few days later, he went out in the morning for one of his regular walks up
the hill near his hotel, and did not return. He was found lying peacefully by
the side of the road, where he had stopped to rest in the morning sunshine.

His elder daughter, Diana, came to arrange the funeral, which was
held quietly at the English church on Malta, with only Colonel Stable and
herself in attendance. [6] When she returned to England, and sorted through
the few possessions he had left behind, she found in each old suit, carefully
pressed and folded away, the small stub of a pencil, sharpened and ready to
use.

SELECT BIBLIOGRAPHY

MAJOR MAGAZINE CONTRIBUTIONS

The Royal: 1904–5
London Opinion: 1904, 1908–23
The Tatler: 1904–7, 1919–36
The Bystander: 1905, 1909–12, 1917, 1923
The Sketch: 1905–14
The Windsor: 1906–8
Pearson's Weekly: 1907
Printers' Pie: 1907–9
Lady's Realm: 1908–10
The Granta: 1910, 1920
The Graphic: 1912, 1920
Punch: 1916–25, 1930–35, 1948
Pan: 1919
Life: 1923

EARLY CONTRIBUTIONS TO COMICS

Scraps: 1903
Comic Life: 1903
Chips: 1903–4

CARTOON COLLECTIONS

Burlesques, with an Introduction by A. E. Johnson (Duckworth, 1916)
A Book of Drawings, with an Introduction by G. K. Chesterton (Methuen, 1921)
Suburbia (Methuen, 1922)
More Drawings (Methuen, 1922)
Adventures at Golf (Methuen, 1923)
A Mixture (Methuen, 1924)
Colonels (Methuen, 1925)
Rebound (Methuen, 1927)
Brought Forward (Methuen, 1931)
Considered Trifles (Hutchinson, 1934)

PROSE WORKS

The Art of Drawing (Methuen, 1926)
Introduction to *Caran d'Ache the Supreme* (Methuen, 1933)
H. M. Bateman by Himself (Collins, 1937)
On the Move in England (Hutchinson, 1940)
The Evening Rise (Duckworth, 1960)

BATEMAN STUDIES

P. V. Bradshaw: *The Art of the Illustrator* (1916)
Michael Bateman (ed.): *The Man Who Drew the Twentieth Century* (Macdonald, 1969)
John Jensen (ed.): *The Man Who . . . and Other Drawings* (Eyre Methuen, 1975)

BOOK ILLUSTRATIONS

William Caine: *Bildad the Quill-Driver* (John Lane, 1916)
Robert K. Risk: *Songs of the Links* (Duckworth, 1919)
George Robey: *After-Dinner Stories* (Grant Richards, 1920)
W. P. Lipscomb: *Staff Tales* (Constable, 1920)
H. M. Walbrook: *Gilbert and Sullivan Opera* (F. V. White, 1922)
Langford Reed: *The Complete Limerick Book* (Jarrolds, 1924)
Desmond Coke: *Our Modern Youth* (Chapman & Hall, 1924)
Langford Reed: *Nonsense Verses* (Jarrolds, 1925)
Dudley Clark: *Bateman and I in Filmland* (Fisher Unwin, 1926)
Langford Reed (ed.): *Further Nonsense Verse and Prose*, Lewis Carroll (Fisher Unwin, 1926)
William Caine: *What a Scream!* (Phillip Allan, 1927)
Geoffrey Dowd: *Whiffs from the Briny* (Heath Cranton, 1931)
R. D. Peck: *Fly-Fishing for Duffers* (A. & C. Black, 1934)
A. P. Herbert: *Dolphin Square* (Richard Costain, 1935)
'A Member of Tattersalls': *Tales of the Turf and Ring* (World's Work, 1936)
R. D. Peck: *Spinning for Duffers* (A. & C. Black, 1939)
Jan Gordon: *Art Ain't All Paint* (Feature Books, 1944)
George Brennard: *Walton's Delight* (Michael Joseph, 1953)

NOTES

PREFACE

1 Batemen Estate.
2 R. G. G. Price: *A History of 'Punch'* (Collins, 1957)
3 Bernard Hollowood: *Pont* (Collins, 1969)
4 John Lewis: *Heath Robinson* (Constable, 1973)
5 *H. M. Bateman by Himself* (Collins, 1937). Unless otherwise indicated, all Bateman quotations in this study are from his autobiography.
6 David Cuppleditch: *The London Sketch Club* (Dilke Press, 1978), *The John Hassall Lifestyle* (Dilke Press, 1979) and *Phil May: The Artist and His Wit* (Fortune Press, 1981)
7 John Jensen (ed.): *The Man Who ... and Other Drawings* (Eyre Methuen, 1975)

CHAPTER 1

1 Letter to Mrs Brenda Bateman: April 1939
2 Dennis Gifford: *The British Comic Catalogue 1874–1974* (Mansell, 1975)
3 David Low: *An Autobiography* (Michael Joseph, 1956)
4 Michael Bateman (ed.): *The Man Who Drew the Twentieth Century* (Macdonald, 1969)
5 It was produced under the care of Dalziel Bros, the leading firm of engravers who had worked for most of the best illustrative artists of the period. Among the artists who drew for *Fun* were Bernard Partridge, M. Greiffenhagen, F. Catchpole, and J. F. Sullivan.
6 Whistler said that black-and-white art could be summed up in two words: 'Phil May.'
7 Bateman Estate.
8 William Heath Robinson: *My Line of Life* (Langton Day, 1938)
9 Introduction to V. & A. catalogue: *An Exhibition of Modern Illustration* (1901)
10 Op. cit.
11 James Thorpe, illustrator and cartoonist, and a close friend of Bateman, gives a good explanation of the new processes in *Phil May: Master Draughtsman and Humorist, 1864–1903* (Harrap, 1932).

> The construction of a line block may be explained briefly as a mechanical development of the process of etching. The drawing is photographed in reverse on to a zinc plate covered with a sensitized gelatine film. The lines are protected against the action of acid, which is used to eat away the exposed portions, or the 'whites' of the drawing, leaving the artist's lines raised in relief. The metal plate is then backed with wood and can be printed from in the same way as and simultaneously with ordinary type.

> For half-tone blocks, which are generally of copper, the illustration is photographed through a glass screen, with fine lines of varying mesh drawn across in both directions. This breaks up the photograph into a series of dots of different degrees of size and closeness, thus producing a close approximation to the graduated depths of tone in the original.

He goes on to suggest why it was that so many artists during the 1890s, on the introduction of the new processes, turned away from the representational towards the humorous and decorative.

> The development of the half-tone block also facilitated the reproduction of photographs, and here time took its revenge, for the initial cost of photographs was far less, and they gradually took the place of drawings: and so the process which had at first encouraged the draughtsman presently threatened to extinguish him. Today the pictorial record of news is almost entirely in the hands of photographers.

12 The firm of Dalziel Bros went broke in 1893. They claimed their losses were due to 'the extinction of their wood-engraving business, owing to the introduction of automatic processes.' Simon Houfe: *The Dictionary of British Book Illustrators and Caricaturists 1800–1914.* (Antique Collectors Club, 1978), to which excellent book I owe much of the information and many of the ideas here.
13 Ibid. The list of contributors to the V. & A. exhibition reads like a roll call of honour, and shows the enormous depth of talent in England in black-and-white art during the period 1860–1900. It includes, alphabetically: E. A. Abbey, Baden-Powell, Aubrey Beardsley, F. Brangwyn, C. and H. Brock, Ford Madox Brown, Burne-Jones, Walter Crane, Ralph Caldecott, Philip Connard, George Cruikshank, Frank Dadd, Richard Doyle, George du Maurier, Harry Furniss, Charles Dana Gibson, Kate Greenaway, M. Greiffenhagen, Dudley Hardy, John Hassall, Laurence Housman, William Holman Hunt, Charles Keene, John Leech, Frederick Leighton, Alberto Martini, Phil May, William Morris, Henry Ospovat, Bernard Partridge, Fred Pegram, J. Pennell, Phiz (Halbôt Brown), Lucien Pissarro, Arthur Rackham, L. Raven-Hill, Charles Ricketts, Dante Gabriel Rossetti, Linley Sambourne, Fred Sandys, Byam

Shaw, Claude A. Shepperson, S. H. Sime, J. F. Sullivan, Sir John Tenniel, W. M. Thackeray, Hugh Thompson, Daniel Vierge, G. F. Watts, J. McNeill Whistler, and J. B. Yeats.

CHAPTER 2

1 There was, around the turn of the century, a considerable expansion in the number of art schools in London – over sixty-five in 1895. This was partly due to the increased interest in, and democratization of, artistic matters through magazines – especially *The Studio*, with its competitions for budding artists, and many surveys of the contemporary scene. See T. MacKenzie (ed.): *The Art Schools of London* (V. & A., 1895)

2 *The Tatler* was in fact founded in 1709 – Clement Shorter founded *The Sphere*.

3 See Cuppleditch: *Phil May*

4 *The Studio*, Vol. 36

5 Ibid.

6 The connections between individual artists in England and the continental schools and studios are fascinating but somewhat labyrinthine. For example, Hassall studied in Paris under Bougereau, who also taught Hardy, the Beggerstaff Brothers (James Pryde and William Nicholson) and Raven-Hill, the *Punch* cartoonist. See Houfe: op. cit.

7 Hassall openly acknowledged his debt to Cheret, and was somewhat despairing about the inimical conditions in England. He wrote in an article for *Pearson's Weekly*, 'About Posters,' in 1905: 'The poster is, of course, new in England. Indeed, I find on consulting my dictionary that the word "poster" is not yet recognized by modern Johnsons, although surely it is preferable to the cumbrous "pictorial placard" or the French word "*affiche*," excellently descriptive as that is. . . .

'Jules Cheret, the doyen and master of all poster artists, was the first to introduce the poster to the man in the street, and to this day the highest form of poster art is Parisian.

'My friend Mr Dudley Hardy was the first to awaken advertisers to the value of high-class pictorial posters with his splendid designs for *Gaiety Girl* and *Today*, and since then the popularity of the poster has increased with enormous strides, and they have become more and more artistic. But in artistic merit they still fall far short of French work.' See Cuppleditch: *Hassall*.

CHAPTER 3

1 Of Van Havermaet and his studio little is known, nor is it certain who were the two or three other students Bateman mentions in his autobiography as

his companions. It seems probable that A. R. Thomson, the deaf and dumb artist, a friend and fellow member of the Chelsea Arts Club, was one. Cuppleditch, in his book on Hassall, says that Bert Thomas and Harry Rountree were also pupils there, but exactly when and for how long is not known. According to Houfe (op. cit.) Rountree studied with Percival Gaskell at the Regent Street Polytechnic. It seems that Hassall took over the studio in 1908, after Bateman had left, and called it the New Art School and School of Poster Design, but this may have been an entirely different venture, since, while both places were in the Earls Court area, there are some discrepancies in the exact addresses. A. E. Johnson, in *The Book of Hassall* (one of his *Brush, Pen and Pencil* series, published in 1907), wrote, 'And to his other activities John Hassall adds those of teacher, for he is one of the principals of the London School of Art, Stratford Studios, Stratford, London.'

2 P. V. Bradshaw: *The Art of the Illustrator*: Bateman portfolio (1916).

3 Bateman's boxing cartoons form a considerable body of work, and perhaps the best date from the early 1920s, long after he had given up active participation in the sport.

CHAPTER 4

1 These were namely *The Tatler*, *The Sketch*, *London Opinion*, *Pearson's Weekly*, *Printers' Pie*, and *The Windsor*.

2 One thinks of Charles Keene, John Leech, Sir John Tenniel, Linley Sambourne, George du Maurier, Bernard Partridge and company.

3 A. J. Munnings: *An Artist's Life*, Vol. 2: 'The Second Burst' (Museum Press, 1951).

4 J. B. Priestley: *The Edwardians* (Heinemann, 1970)

5 Price: op. cit.

6 Oliver Onions: *The Work of Henry Ospovat* (St Catherine Press, 1911)

7 *The Studio*, Vol. 53, 1911. George Sheringham: 1884–1937.

8 Frank Hart (1878–1959) became godfather to Bateman's younger daughter, Monica.

CHAPTER 5

1 Cuppleditch: *Sketch Club*.

2 *The Studio*, Vol. 30,

3 In the 1908 exhibition Bateman had three paintings: 'The Ray' (nine guineas), 'Beachcombers' (six guineas) and 'Vespers' (five guineas). I have been unable to trace any of these. See London Sketch Club Library: *Long Ago*.

4   H. M. Bateman: unpublished essay on London
    Sketch Club (Bateman Estate).

5   H. M. Bateman: 'The Old London Sketch Club'
    (*The Artist*, 1968)

6   T. H. H. Hancock: letter to the author.

7   The Minute Books, the Register of Members, and
    the Candidate Books of the Chelsea Arts Club are in
    Chelsea Library, Kings Road, London.

8   *London Opinion*, July 15, 1911.

CHAPTER 6

1   T. W. H. Crosland: *The Suburbans* (Long, 1905)

2   Donald Read: *Edwardian England 1901–1915:
    Society and Politics* (Harrap, 1972)

3   A. J. P. Taylor: *History of England 1914–1945*
    (O.U.P., 1965)

4   Read: op. cit.

5   Ibid. Contemporary music hall song.

6   Robert Cecil: *Life in Edwardian England*
    (Batsford, 1969)

7   William Caine: *The Glutton's Mirror*
    (Fisher Unwin, 1925)

8   Ibid.

9   Cornelius Veth: *Comic Art in England*
    (Edward Goldston, 1930)

CHAPTER 7

1   David Low: *British Cartoonists, Caricaturists and
    Comic Artists* (Collins, 1942).

2   Ibid.

3   Read: op. cit.

4   Ibid.

5   John Dickson Carr: *Life of Sir Arthur Conan Doyle*
    (Murray, 1949).

CHAPTER 8

1   *The Sketch*, October 1912.

2   Monocle on Bateman.

3   Monocle on Chelsea Arts Ball.

4   Bateman on G.B.S.

5   See H. M. Bateman: *The Evening Rise* (Duckworth,
    1960).

CHAPTER 9

1   Rupert Brooke: 'Peace' (1914)

2   Read: op. cit.

3   Op. cit.

4   Bateman was, of course, by no means alone in his
    misery and disturbance. C. G. F. Masterman, in his
    great book *England after the War* (Hodder &
    Stoughton, 1922) quoted the American Ambas-
    sador to London, a Dr Page, who said in 1916, 'You
    will recall more clearly than I certain horrible,
    catastrophic, universal ruin passages in Revelations
    – monsters swallowing the universe, blood and fire

and clouds and an eternal crash, rotting ruin
enveloping all things ... There are perhaps ten
million men dead of this war and perhaps a hundred
million persons to whom death would be a blessing.
Add to these as many millions more whose views of
life are so distorted that blank idiocy would be a
better mental outlook, and you'll get a hint (and
only a hint) of what this continent has already
become – a bankrupt slaughterhouse inhabited by
unmated women. We have talked of "problems" in
our day. We never had a problem: for the worst task
we ever saw was a mere blithe pastime compared
with what these women and the few men that will
remain here must face. The hills about Verdun are
not blown to pieces worse than the social structure
and intellectual and spiritual life of Europe. I
wonder that anybody is sane.'

5   Stephen Graham: Foreword to Caine: op. cit.

6   Bert Thomas, who drew for *Punch* from 1905 to
    1935, but not in 1916, was also a brilliant
    draughtsman, and, although perhaps less original
    than Bateman, a great cartoonist.

CHAPTER 10

1   The magazine was called *Simplicissimus* because the
    French magazine *Gil Blas*, upon which it was
    modelled, took its name from the picaresque novel
    by Alain René Lesage, and Simplicissimus was the
    name of the eponymous hero of a seventeenth-
    century German picaresque novel, *Der Abenteuer-
    liche Simplicissimus Teutsch*, by J. J. C. von Grim-
    melshausen (whose work was also the inspiration
    for Brecht's *Mother Courage*). Simplicissimus
    pretended to be a court jester, and castigated the
    failings of his listeners. See Stanley Appelbaum
    (ed.): *Simplicissimus: 180 Satirical Drawings*
    (Dover, 1975). Appelbaum calls the German
    weekly 'one of the greatest picture magazines in the
    history of journalism.' Founded in 1896, it
    appeared until 1944, then from 1954 until 1967,
    when it ceased publication.

2   *Strand Magazine*, Vol. 15.

3   Ibid.

4   Bateman was not alone in England, either, in using
    a Caran d'Ache-influenced strip cartoon form, or in
    seeing the comic possibilities inherent in the violent
    denouement. Both Fougasse and Heath Robinson
    drew memorable cartoons of this kind. Fougasse's
    'Lady impaling the man in front of her at the
    theatre with a hatpin' and Heath Robinson's 'Man
    at a restaurant mistaking the bald head of his
    neighbour for a Dutch cheese and taking a slice out
    of it' are two notable examples.

5   H. M. Bateman: Introduction to *Caran d'Ache the
    Supreme* (Methuen, 1933).

CHAPTER 11

1 *The Bookman*, December 1922.
2 Bradshaw: op. cit.
3 John Arlott essay: 'Sport': S. Nowell-Smith (ed.): *Edwardian England 1901–1914* (O.U.P., 1964)
4 Robert K. Risk: *Songs of the Links* (Duckworth, 1919).
5 John Bohun Lynch: *A History of Caricature* (Faber & Gwyer, 1926).
6 Op. cit.
7 Frank Reynolds: *Humorous Drawing for the Press* (Methuen, 1947).
8 Bradshaw: op. cit. Caricatures of George Grossmith, a popular comedian, perhaps best remembered now for his writing, in collaboration with his brother, Weedon, the comic masterpiece *Diary of a Nobody*.
9 *Journal of the Royal Society of Arts*, 1949. Osbert Lancaster was in the chair for Bateman's lecture.
10 H. M. Bateman: untitled essay on the function of the artist. Bateman Estate.
11 Ibid.

CHAPTER 12

1 Bateman Estate.
2 Munnings: op. cit.

CHAPTER 13

1 Bevis Hillier (ed.): *Fougasse* (Elm Tree, 1977)
2 See Fougasse's 'Man Who sneezed in front of the Solo Violinist.'
3 A. A. Milne: *It's Too Late Now* (Methuen, 1939)
4 John Galsworthy: *Swan Song* (Heinemann, 1928).
5 Ibid.
6 H. M. Bateman: 'Success' (unpublished essay). Bateman Estate.

CHAPTER 14

1 *Christian Science Monitor*, March 14, 1921.
2 H. M. Bateman: *Homes from Home* (unpublished manuscript). Bateman Estate.
3 Ibid.
4 H. M. Bateman: 'What I Thought of New York' (*Pall Mall*, September 1923).
5 It is not clear if Bateman's drawings were ever used. I have not been able to trace the advertisements. George Hill spent something like $250,000 on promoting Lucky Strike cigarettes, and Bateman was merely a part of this massive advertising campaign.
6 *Homes from Home*.
7 I am indebted to John Jensen for this information about the *New Yorker*.

CHAPTER 15

1 In fact, his very last cartoons appeared in *Punch* in 1948, after a gap of 14 years. It is rather doubtful, however, that these cartoons – two of them – were actually drawn at that time, being probably productions of the 1930s, used by Bateman at the later date. He sometimes did this: for instance, the cartoon 'The Drive,' though published in 1932, was actually produced in 1912.
2 Bateman had throughout the 1920s provided a steady stream of illustrations for various books (see Bibliography) and magazine articles, and this continued during the 1930s and beyond. This was, however, always a very minor mode, and not always a successful one.
3 In the late 1920s and early 1930s he was earning about £5,000 p.a.
4 Letters to Mrs Brenda Bateman and Mrs Monica Pine.
5 Letter to Mrs Brenda Bateman.
6 Letter to Mrs Brenda Bateman.
7 H. M. Bateman: *World Tour* (unpublished manuscript). Bateman Estate.
8 H. M. Bateman: *On the Move In England* (Hutchinson, 1940).
9 *Oxford Mail*, February 16, 1943.
10 Mrs Monica Pine: letter to the author.

CHAPTER 16

1 H. M. Bateman: 'The Other Man' (unpublished story). Bateman Estate.
2 H. M. Bateman: untitled and unpublished essay. Bateman Estate.
3 H. M. Bateman: another untitled and unpublished essay. Bateman Estate.

CHAPTER 17

1 George Brennard: *Walton's Delight* (Michael Joseph, 1953)
2 Letter to Mrs Monica Pine.
3 Letter to Mrs Monica Pine.
4 Vivien Noakes: *Edward Lear* (Collins, 1968)
5 Letter to Mrs Monica Pine.
6 Bateman's funeral contained elements of comedy that were almost tragic. Appropriately for such an unhumorous humorist, the whole solemn affair was continually punctured by the ridiculous and the chaotic.
   His wish was to be cremated, his ashes scattered over some part of the Gozithan countryside, but owing to complications with the authorities in Malta this was not allowed. Instead he had to be transported to Malta and buried in the Protestant church there. On the day of his removal many

friends, both native and expatriate, gathered by the quayside to bid him farewell.

His daughter, Diana, and Colonel Stable rode with the coffin in a horse-drawn vehicle from the hotel down the hill to the waiting boat. It was a steep hill, and the horse seemed incapable of coping with the weight and kept breaking into a sliding run which threatened to debouch all the occupants prematurely upon the roadside.

Having at last been safely conveyed into the boat, a small open vessel, they put out for Malta. No sooner had they cleared the harbour than a storm brewed up and waves came crashing into the boat. The rest of the journey was a nightmare: the open part of the boat in which Diana and Colonel Stable sat with the coffin was covered with a tarpaulin, and they had to complete the trip in total darkness on a very rough sea. At last they arrived and made their way to the church. It was shut. So the vicar was searched for and found, and finally Bateman was buried peacefully and with dignity after a simple but moving ceremony.

Monica, who had to come from Canada for the funeral, arrived the day after, her plane delayed.

Perhaps the only comment Bateman himself might have made upon the whole affair would have been a cartoon: 'The Man Who tried to have his Remains disposed of in accordance with his own Wishes.'

ACKNOWLEDGEMENTS

I would like to thank Christopher Willoughby for all the meticulous and painstaking photographic work he has done on the reproductions for this book. I would also like to thank the staffs of the British Library, the Victoria and Albert Museum Library and the Westminster Art Library who all helped so willingly with my queries, Marianne Bonney, Librarian of the *Punch* Library, for her help and kindness, and the writers and publishers of all those books upon which I drew for background historical information, such as A. J. P. Taylor, Donald Read, Simon Houfe, J. B. Priestley and Alan Jenkins.

I would also like to thank the following for their permission to reproduce cartoons: British Library 92, 108; Dennis Gifford and The Dennis Gifford Comic Library 11; the proprietors of *Punch*; the proprietors of *The Tatler*.

INDEX

Page numbers in italic type refer to illustrations
n indicates a reference to the Notes